"If we laugh, we live."
– Constantinople Ob

The Ob-servations of Constantinople Ob

The Ob-servations of Constantinople Ob

Compiled,
Catalogued
and Edited
By

JOHN THOM

This book is a product of **Bat & Ball Press**. Other books from **Bat & Ball Press** include the already published and forthcoming novels in the Jaguar Beault Thriller series:
The Madagascar Pigeon (2014)
Termination Determinators (2015)
The Nuclear Armageddon Endgame (2015)

Evil In Silicon Valley (2016)
"Citizen Beault" (2017, if the creek don't rise)

Order Bat & Ball Press Books:
Print copies from **Amazon.com**
E-reader version on your **Kindle**

Contact the publisher at jaguarbeault@gmail.com

ISBN-13: 9780961124243
ISBN-10: 0961124245
Library of Congress Control Number: 2015916363

Bat & Ball Press
San Francisco

A note about the publisher: **Bat & Ball Press** opened for business in the 1980s when it issued the second best book ever written in the vast library of baseball history, entitled ***Champion Batsmen of the 20th Century***. That was a time before the steroid plague sullied the game and many of its hitting and pitching stars. All the employees of **Bat & Ball Press**, great fans of the game, lost their innocence and sadly – but filled with confidence – set out to find a new voice in the publishing game. They found that voice in the Jaguar Beault Thrillers. Jaguar Beault does not do steroids. It is nature that dealt him his imposing size and strength, not banned supplements used by cheaters. Constantinople Ob now joins the stable of writers at **Bat & Ball Press** making publishing history. There is no evidence that Ob intentionally does – or has done – steroids. Certainly his unimposing stature suggests he would not know an HGH if it hit him in his mouth. **Bat & Ball Press** moved from Los Angeles to San Francisco and has not looked back.

Table of Contents

Preface

By John Thom

(Read this first. It will help you more readily understand this book. Not that it will be all that hard if you don't read this first. It will just be easier, believe me. Well, do as you please; it was your money that paid for the book. The Preface is going to start now.)

When work on *Word for Word* was nearly finished, I discovered that one of my co-editors was an accomplished essayist. His worldview was ideally suited to the dictionary wherein he could add insights and observations that would be elucidative of the definitions in *Word for Word*. He was Constantinople Ob. Actually, he still is.

What is *Word for Word* you ask, and well you should, elsewise you won't know. *Word for Word* is the still unpublished abridged dictionary of unabridged value a bunch of us worked on. Unpublished, yes, and another instance of the myopia rampant throughout the literary landscape. Afflicted are book agents and publishers. Otherwise you and the rest of the reading public would even now have a copy in your book stacks, another on your desktop and one in your business office. (If you worked in an office.) Well, you don't. You don't have a copy because of that "unpublished" condition of the book. Timid and short-sighted fools. Not you, the agents and publishers.

Consequently, I convinced C. Ob that we collect some of his Ob-servations into a single volume. Here it is thanks to a less myopic publisher. (The Preface is over.) (No, it isn't.) I forgot to mention that references to a blog are to one that C. Ob posted to. A few of these Ob-servations appeared there. As there are about 780 billion blogs in cyberspace and you can't read more than two or three a day, the chances that you saw his blog are slim. Probably none. Just wanted you to know that. (Now the Preface is over.) (Nuts, still not over. I have to mention something, so keep going.) This volume honors the memory of Robert Benchley with deserved admiration and heartfelt appreciation because a book of his delightful writings that came into my possession at a library sale was the spark that re-ignited the little literary fire and the comic warmth that glows in my soul and, I hope, in these pages. I trust you share that warmth. (There! Now the Preface is really over. If I think of anything else to say, well, I won't say it.)

The Ob-servations Themselves

Self-Cleaning

You had to be there to know the specifics of that moment when someone got the idea of a self-cleaning oven. I was not there. I was probably taking a nap. People who take naps at critical, life-changing moments generally do not conceive life-changing ideas. This in no way should be taken as a dig at naps. Naps have a place in the progression of ideas. Likely as not, however, it's after the heavy lifting has been done toward the good idea. A kind of reward.

Think about it. A self-cleaning oven. Who would have thought about such a thing? Shoot, I asked that wrong. I know who *would* have. I should have asked who *could* have thought about such a thing. Who *could* have was a really smart person. Who *would* have would have been my mother. She cooks. And she uses an oven on occasion. And on those occasions the oven builds up residues from the food and it gets dirty. Then the oven needs cleaning.

Before self-cleaning ovens, kitchens, where most ovens are, were stocked with sponges, ammonia, steel wool, and other devices and solutions to wipe away grease and grit and odors from the oven. Our kitchen was so stocked, though it lacked one thing that would be found in most other kitchens. My father. Dad was more inclined to eat in the kitchen than to clean in there. He also had a favorite chair, his books and newspaper, his collection of 78's, and his "medicinal" concoctions. But enough about dad.

How does it work anyway? How does an oven clean itself? There is no brush inside it. No acids. No live-in maid. You push a button and set a timer and come back in a while to a clean oven. Or so they say. When you get right down to it, it doesn't make sense, and to support that, let me ask you this, mister know-it-all, where does the dirt go? Dirty oven one minute, clean oven the next and no bag to toss in the trash. There's only one answer. The whole idea is bunk. It sure makes for a great sales gimmick. You see it in ads. "America's self-cleaning oven." You get the same message from the floorwalker. "It cleans itself." You're tempted to buy two it sounds so good. Only then do you recall that your kitchen has room for just one. That was a close call.

You never did ask how this self-cleaning gets done, did you? You've got to be more assertive. Interrogate that floorwalker. Push him into a corner for the answers. Do not settle for "I'm only the salesman." They always try that one on you. Demand to speak to a supervisor. I've said it before and I'll say it again – I don't know why I have to think of everything.

If you really want to know how it's done, this self-cleaning oven feature, you'll need to ask the inventor. When you do and you're getting all this technobabble and double talk, tell him you won't believe in "self-cleaning" until he comes up with an invention where he cannot get away with "Oh, it's clean all right, you just have to look real close." Ha, I say to that. Tell him you will believe in his idea when he invents one where the results will not only be very visible, but also very much more useful – the self-cleaning garage.

The Dog Assignments

The line started here and meandered a long way, so long that one would not see its end though one stood on top of something. Even then one would need outstanding eyesight with superb depth perception. But this is not about the line. Or eyes. This is about why all the people were in the line.

The line was for dog assignments. At the business end of the line in a shed with a desk, a chair and an issuer, every human being on Earth was assigned his or her dog. "Everybody gets a dog," the dog issuer behind the desk snapped when confronted with an objection to the rule. "Take it up with the guy in charge," he snapped again when the complainant pressed ahead that he or she wanted to decline a dog. No, he did not know where the guy in charge was, "I just issue the dogs."

The rule came about when the guy in charge was on his daily walk one morning in his neighborhood – his own dog on a leash – and discovered that at one residence there was a noticeable silence because there was no barking. "What-what?" the guy in charge reacted. He stepped back to look down the driveway. No car. More to the point, however, no gate. No gate? No place to hang the "Beware of Dog" sign. The guy in charge gasped at the possibility. No dog? "Ah," he concluded, "inside and asleep. A frisky pup past his playtime and now at rest." Or else there would be barking as at virtually every other house and apartment building along his walk.

Case closed.

Not quite. On a subsequent morning and a subsequent walk the guy in charge happened to meet the same residence's resident. After exchanging pleasantries, the guy in charge remarked innocently, "Have any pets?"

"Oh, sure, we're animal lovers."

Relieved, the guy in charge asked expectantly, "What's your dog's name?"

"Queenie, only she's not a dog, she's a cat."

The guy in charge did not exactly clutch at his heart. He did make a mental note on the sad episode. Then he went home and wrote the brochure. He put everything into the brochure. The brochure is called *Dog Rules*. He reasoned that was more appropriate than *Dogs Rule*.

The line moved slowly. Well, the "line" didn't move, people in it moved. They moved toward the shed slowly because there were delays with each new issuing chore.

"But I don't want a dog."

"Good grief, everybody gets a dog. It's the rule. Move along."

And…"Do you have a St. Bernard?"

"You get what I give you."

"I want a St. Bernard."

"You get…geez, I hate this job…you get what's next on the list. Move along."

And…"I don't have room for a dog."

"Not my problem. You get a dog. It's the rule. Move along."

And…"I'm allergic to dander."

"So? You want a medal?"

"But I'm allergic."

"Hold on." At this the dog issuer got out of his chair and walked around his desk to the shed door. Opening it, he stepped onto the porch and shouted, "Doesn't anyone read the brochure? Read the damn brochure. It's got the rules in it. Geez." A few people near the front of the line pulled the brochure out of their pockets.

"Rules are rules," the dog issuer mumbled to himself as he went back into his shed. "What are they, bloody illiterates? Whew, I'm glad I got that off my chest. You, yes you, move along." For a few minutes the line moved less slowly (the people in it) and that made the dog issuer less grumpy. Until…

"I get a dog, what do I do now?" a customer asked the dog issuer.

"Take this coupon to that line over there," he said, pointing out through a side window.

"What's the coupon for?"

Another illiterate, he thought. "It's for a pooper scooper. Didn't you read the brochure?"

"A what?"

"Don't worry, it comes with instructions. Have someone read them to you."

"It sounds disgusting."

"It is disgusting, but you get used to it."

"A dog I don't want, a pooper scooper that turns me off, a barking machine that will keep me awake all night. I am really starting to resent his. What other surprises should I look ahead to?"

"Let me see. Oh, you got a male. You better plan to wear long pants all the time. He's not fixed."

"This sucks, man. Why don't you and the guy in charge go straight to hell?"

The dog issuer looked up at the customer. "Too late. Why do you think I have this job?"

DNR

DNR. Those are bold and brave letters. DNR. "Do Not Resuscitate." Bold and brave. You – we'll call you Jack – come tumbling down a hill and you smack your head on a rock and you are knocked senseless. Your friend – let's call her Jill – comes tumbling down after and rams into your back snapping your spine and paralyzing you from the cowlick on the top of your head down to your toenails. Someone dials 9-1-1 and a paramedic crew arrives bent on saving your life. That's what they do. That's what they train for. That's what they're paid to do. They might even take oaths to do just that. I don't know. About the oath part. They whip out their specialized equipment and start saving your life.

Until your lawyer shows up holding that DNR he prepared for you and the very one you signed when you could manipulate a pen and when you were certain that you were immune to the hazards on that hill including Jill's clumsiness.

Not me. When my lawyer shows up he will not have a DNR to wave in the faces of paramedics and doctors. My attorney will have an R. "Resuscitate." Even better…an RN. "Resuscitate Now." I am going to want the medicos to plug me into every machine they have in the hospital. Oxygen, blood sera, tubes of all descriptions, IVs in both arms and both legs, bath immersions. Whatever they can put their hands on. I'll even want them to run a power line from the local electric utility company right through my window into my brain.

"Do Not Resuscitate." Whoever heard of such a thing? What if it's just a passing spasm? "Oh, sorry, Ob family and friends, we thought he was terminal, not that it was just a passing spasm, and that his RN was just a misprint. He could have lasted another 40 or 50 years." A misprint? They go to college for four years and medical school for another three years and they intern for a couple more, then they walk into my room and they can't read? A "misprint"? Godfrey Daniel.

Maybe a tattoo is the answer: "Resuscitate Me As Fast As You Can." Two of 'em, actually. One across my chest and one on my forehead.

No Clues

There is this board game where you, like, have to say who did, you know, a murder or something, and, I mean, where it happened and with, like, what weapon. Guess what, there's like no clues. How bogus is that? Guess what, the game it's called Clue. "Clue!" Yeaw. Where's, like, some clues, dude?

Why am I dictating like this? I have no idea. I'll take a breath.

Back to Clue. Playing the game taught me a lesson to remember. It is that I would make a truly dreadful detective. While other players practically eye-witnessed the crime, I am just eliminating my first suspect because her card is in my pile. Which room? No idea. Weapon? Don't ask me. Even if I heard a gunshot I'd be in the dark about the murder implement.

All of which leads to the sad admission that I once had dreams of being a private eye. The work environment appealed to me: underworld characters; inept cops; victims needing the skill set of the problem solver; dames; forty dollars a day and expenses; a neat hat; a car conversant with the noir environment of private eyes.

But it was not to be and will not now. One good thing is that at forty dollars a day it was pretty certain that I would reach poverty before I nabbed my first scofflaw. The honest truth? I didn't need to finish last in a Clue tournament to recognize my failings at ratiocination. Realization came long before.

It was on a ride-along. Our local police force from time to time allowed interested citizens to accompany a police unit on a shift, often at night when the prospects were better for criminal behavior. I was an interested citizen. Interested...though embarrassingly uninformed about real police work.

Along about midnight our car got a call. There was an unmistakable rush of relief from the front seat. "Two Blue Four Uniform, code three to north parking lot at Dan Quayle Park. Gunshots reported."

Gunshots? Holy Satan's socks! Gunshots? As I began to outline my understanding of the parameters of a police ride-along to the two officers and how gunshots did not enter into any description ("Why do you think we carry guns?" one of the comedians grinned at me from the front seat) the cops rechecked their seat belts as we Nascarred down the avenue.

Dan Quayle was a U.S. vice president. He was from another state. Why the park is named in his honor I do not know. What is so special about the north parking lot I do not know. Why the need for our police unit at the north parking lot and where the lot even is I do not know. Okay, gunshots reported.

At an undetermined time between the first radio call and our arrival at the appointed place, I, uh, lost consciousness. Yes, I know, most unmanly. Hey, I'd like to see how you would react under the same circumstances. Let it also be noted that the last food I had was at the diner about three hours earlier. Low blood sugar.

Okay, there it is. The reason Con Ob will not seek fame, fortune and adventure as a gumshoe. I don't watch police shows on television anymore either.

"Ob"

Does this happen to you? It happens to me and I wonder just what serendip-ity has passed through my hands all these years. Well, not all these years. It's probably just a few, but exaggeration comes to mind when you are agitated with yourself.

What happened was I would get my mail each day and flip through it making quick decisions about each piece. You know, a bill goes here to be paid, a post card goes there to be taped to the refrigerator, and this one goes in the waste bin.

The waste bin. And that is just the problem. What treasures, I ask myself now, have I lackadaisically deposited in the waste bin with no more attention than that I was not interested. I repeat, does this happen to you? You'll be thankful now that I am bringing this to your attention so that, like me, you will mend your ways.

For me the light went on over my head when I was flipping through that day's mail and I stopped at a brochure from my local adult education campus. Well, not *my* adult education campus because I'd been disclaiming the place for a long time by my inattention to the brochures. It was in my neighbor-hood though.

In the event, the brochure practically said, "Hey, what about me?" And I said, "What's all this then?" I was taken in. I am glad to say that the brochure, actually a catalog of classes offered for the next term, had me in its clutches.

I tossed down all my other mail and began perusing the catalog. I was fascinated, but tossing down my other mail proved to be a costly distraction because there were several bills in the pile that did not get timely consid-eration and later on there was a stink about overdue payments. I managed through that okay because I had a new sense of divertissement, this adult education program.

I'm not going to go into any long treatment about the choices of classes available and how hard it was to pick a course. I had about six weeks before classes were to begin and I used up nearly all that time trying to decide.

The class I chose met two times a week at night from seven to ten. I was not the first student to arrive on the first night, but there were desks available and I sat down. The teacher was there before me and was waiting at his own desk at the front of the classroom. He was reading quietly. At seven, he stood and offered a nice welcome. "First things first," he announced, saying, "I need to take roll." In just a short interval he got to the O's.

"Ob," he said, looking up.

"Here," I answered.

"Ob?"

"Yes?"

"No, I mean is that how it's pronounced?"

"Ob," I said, the way I've said it all my life.

"What kind of name is that?"

"It's my last name."

"Then you got short-changed."

"Pardon?"

"It's too bad that wasn't your second-to-last name."

Some of the other students were snickering.

"What kind of name is it, where do you come from?"

"Cleveland, originally."

"What continent is that on?"

Now more of the other students were laughing.

"Is that short for anything?" he asked.

"What?"

"Ob. That sounds like an abbreviation. What was it before, obstetrician? I'd have shortened that too."

Lots of laughter now.

"No, it's always been Ob for all I know."

"That's just precious. Let's see here, what's your first name?"

"Constantinople."

A lot more laughter now.

"Constantinople?" The teacher could barely get it out for his laughing. "You were named after a city? How come, were you born there?"

"No."

"Was your father stationed there in a war or there on business or something?"

"No, I don't think so."

"Constantinople Ob," he chuckled. "I bet the kids made fun of you when you were young. Did they?"

"No."

"What'd you do, tell them your name was Joe Jones?"

Laughter again.

"No."

"What did they call you?"

"Constantinople."

"How long did it take them?"

"Well, from the time that they met me."

"No, I mean how long did it take them to say 'Constantinople' to you. That's a real mouthful, especially for a child.

"I don't know, I forget."

"Well, don't you worry any more about it. Everyone is equal in my classes and you can call yourself anything that pleases you."

"Thank you."

"You're welcome, Istanbul."

The laughter re-ignited. I, for one, did not find that funny.

Cribbage

My cribbage club was invited to "man" the telephones for a night at our local PBS television station during their fund-raising week. It was a real honor for us. We checked our calendars and those who were free signed up.

I say "man" the telephones only because that's an old and time-tested expression used to show economically that people of both genders were at work. No insult is intended. I include this because I want you to know you can put me in the camp of those who are sensitive to the differences between the genders and to the correct language to be used so no one goes away feeling as if they've been disrespected in any way.

I hope also that there are no places where I've written in these Ob-servations where you could accuse me of insensitivity, or even suspect there was any. You know, if you write a hundred words maybe four or five could be flagged by one person or another as potentially offensive. This is one writer who will be among the front ranks of those to keep that type of crafting to a minimum.

The big night arrived and so did both of us from the cribbage club at the television station. Right away I sensed something was wrong because it didn't start off too well. Somehow the people at PBS had got the idea there were more members in the club than is actually the case. A lot more. So when the two of us showed up there was a period of semi-polite conflict. They on their side had expected enough of our members to fill all the chairs where the telephones were. I didn't count the chairs but it looked to be about two dozen.

We don't have two dozen members in our cribbage club.

To make matters worse, the people at PBS hadn't arranged for any other volunteers for that night. It didn't take very long for all of us to see that the evidence pointed to just that. Fortunately, they were able to conscript members of their own station staff to fill in the empty chairs. The fellow who sat in the empty chair next to mine was the fellow who ran the parking lot booth out front and showed us where to park. He spoke enough English to make a good showing that night, raising several hundred dollars for the station.

The fact that we arrived a bit late, the two of us to fill twenty four or so chairs, also seemed to put the people at PBS a bit more on edge. It didn't take a Sherlock Holmes to figure that out. It was palpable. I guess we hadn't given any thought to how much time it would take to learn how to conduct ourselves on the phones, how to take pledges, how to award bonus gifts, how to get names and addresses. There was near panic by the PBS staff.

On these nights for pledge week, the station tends to pull out the best programs they've shown during the year. On this particular night they showed a documentary on the bombing of Pearl Harbor. I've seen it before and it's pretty good.

The station manager, who seemed to be grinding his teeth for most of the night, said to the two of us as we left after our shift, "Pearl Harbor was a day at the beach compared to tonight." I liked the way he depicted the imagery of that historic event, the beaches of the Hawaiian harbor and all. I said call again next year if you want more help. I won't repeat what he said.

(Rebuttal to "Cribbage." Name withheld by request of an official at the PBS station. It is only fair to include his response in this edition of the Ob-servations.)

I speak for every employee, docent, supporter and viewer of our PBS station when I say that Mr. Ob whitewashes the events associated with the particular night when his cribbage club was scheduled to play a prominent part in the pledge week session in question.

How he can take so lightly the financial effects we suffered that evening astounds me and my associates. It was only the passionate persuasion of our legal advisors that prevented us from hauling him into court. Only in the interest of our PBS community who expect us to be above such frays do I hold my anger in check. I cannot in good faith, however, let it end here without relating one instance (of many) that contributed to a near disaster that evening.

During one of the breaks away from our presentation on Pearl Harbor, Mr. Ob and that catastrophe of a person he was escorting apparently thought it would be funny to resort to ham-handed facial muggings when the camera was on the bank of telephone correspondents. There was nothing funny about it. In fact, we had to apologize to irate viewers for days on end after that juvenile behavior. We've had high school students act more maturely than these two idiots.

All this would have disastrously set back fund-raising for our good efforts were it not for the (by contrast) mature audience we serve.

We at PBS remain disappointed at how the two of them used such a dignified and important event to regress to childish actions. We have, however, decided that *Word for Word* and its editor carry no responsibility for Mr. Ob's antics. We hope someone in authority over there can convey to him and that unspeakable acquaintance of his how boorish they have been.

At The Bookstore

What a world of wonder is the local bookstore even when you leave empty-handed like the other day when I purchased no books. I was, however, cloaked in wonderment. The clerk eyed me closely as I left. I think he thought I might be trying to pull a fast one because I was giggling.

Most book titles do not make me laugh. Or giggle. Unlike the other day. Who in his or her right mind, I contemplated, would have an interest in *The Illustrated Guide to Surgery*? A wannabe chest cutter? An ax murderer? Your doctor? Your spouse?

It was sitting right there in plain view. It may be one thing for an amateur to buy a tome that instructs on how to service or repair a lawnmower, but beginning surgery? Slow down! I was tempted to camp out nearby to see who might purchase a copy. Then call the police on him.

Get this, the book was on the bargain table. It was marked down! Sixty percent off! The bookseller was practically in a conspiracy to launch someone on a spree certain to grab headlines. "Here, you, you look poor, come buy this one and be the first on your block to lobotomize a neighbor."

Doctor Jekyll and Mr. Hyde. I do not laugh at that book title. By contrast, I tremble. A laboratory potion turns the learned doc into a creepy scalpel in that one. That was a long time ago. Today some enterprising publisher has marketed a road map to the vital organs and the main blood arteries for any slob who can pony up a few bucks.

These thoughts circled in my head as I walked out of the bookshop. Who among my acquaintances should I keep at a safe distance? Who had I overtly chastised for an improper lane change? Who held a grudge for something I didn't think I had done?

A world of wonderment is a local bookstore. Indeed!

When I reached my parking place I saw a flyer under my windshield wiper. More to wonder about. It invited me to call a number where "Tami" would provide answers via her psychic talents. She could not have been very good at it because otherwise she would have known to save that flyer for a car whose owner did not consider her "profession" a crockpot of cow pies. On the other hand, maybe I should have called her to ask if she knew any of my friends who had dropped out of medical school and harbored unfulfilled surgical ambitions...via a price-reduced illustrated instruction book. Yikes!

Obedience School

Time enough has passed for me to speak about a venture I undertook a while back and not have to fear a repeat of some of the nightmares I had before I finally shut down the business. And yet I might be criticized for not laying this out earlier as a kind of warning to others who might be holding a similar idea.

At first glance the idea seemed to have merit. It was filling a market niche no one else had served. Any business school worth its benefactor's name teaches this: see a market need and fill it for fun and profit. Maybe not in those words exactly but the message resonates.

I called it Ob's Obedience School. For cats. Plenty of people ran dog obedience schools at the time, so the competition in that field kept business slow and profits thin. But no one had a school to train cats. Now, experience tells me, there was a good reason.

Don't start with the jokes. I've heard them all by now even from my so-called friends. What you probably have *not* heard are the various "cons" of the pros and cons of opening a cat obedience school. You should hear them. Out there in my readership are men and women who still sport the grand old American "can-do" attitude. You may be saying, "I can do what Ob couldn't." All I can say to you is...read on.

Pet owners who bring a dog to a dog obedience trainer can easily outline the canine's shortcomings or petulant behavior: barking; jumping up on people's chests; growling at the mailman; messing on carpets. You know the annoying habits.

When owners bring a cat to a cat obedience trainer, they don't know where to begin the list of areas for improvement. So it is up to the trainer (and that meant me because I was alone in this industry) to pick a place to begin. The first week I had between a half dozen and a dozen client cats. Six or twelve, I didn't know because they kept appearing and disappearing all hours of the day and night.

To begin I decided to secure each to a leash to keep them in the school grounds. Don't do this. Cats do not like leashes. Before I learned that about cats, I had to go out and buy some leather leggings to prevent my clients from opening new wounds from my ankles up to above my knees.

Shedding of hair was an obvious trait to try to correct. Cats like to do this on furniture. I had a dark blue couch brought in. When a cat or a few of them had climbed up onto the top and began licking ("bathing") themselves, I interrupted them to put them down onto a tile floor. Cats do not like to be interrupted. If you still have ambitions toward this line of business, I recommend you buy and wear a football helmet. I did. It helped.

Oh, here's another hint: you can forget about scratching poles. Save your money. I had them positioned around the school in strategic spots where they'd be easily seen. Never used. Why? Because cats scratch wherever they darn well please. You'd know that if you could see my furniture.

I thought potty training would be a snap. If I didn't know much about cats when I started the business, I did know that cats tend to be clean. I took another trip to the store to buy a plastic container and a few bags of kitty litter. Cat A used it. A good start. Cat B, however, disdained it. Cats apparently are protective of their rights about litter boxes. Cat B went under the dark blue couch. Cats C through E went outdoors never to return. Back to the store to get a number more of those plastic containers and a pickup truck load of kitty litter.

Thinking I might kill two cats with one, excuse me, kill two birds with one stone, I placed all those new litter boxes next to all of my scratching poles. My assessment of the uselessness of scratching poles did not change.

At some point I decided to take the initiative and go positive with all my clients. I decided to teach them tricks. Starting off with something simple, I tried "rolling over." I got a 12-inch ruler and motioned one of the cats to "roll over." It just laid there. Nudging it with the ruler in the direction of the "roll over" is not recommended. Cats don't want to "roll over" and, what's more, they don't like to be nudged with a stick. The gashes in my right forearm (I am right-handed) were much deeper than the ones in my left arm.

I was about to go out and buy a leather jacket to protect my arms when I had an epiphany. To heck, I said, with cat obedience training. It is a dead-end street. I telephoned each of my pet owners to admit defeat and to have them come retrieve their cats. Of the eleven I telephoned, only two bothered to show up. And those two I had to give a full refund.

Needle

It all started on a bustling, sun-bathed Saturday afternoon on a downtown street while I was out looking for a store where I could buy a replacement needle for my record player. Those things wear out so I came to discover. The needles do, and they can damage your LPs and 45s if you aren't attentive.

I passed any number of shops with wares of all descriptions. Except record player needles. I began to suspect that the technology had been superseded by audio tapes and CDs and those little gadgets everyone seems to have glued to their hands with wires into their ears. What a discouraging thought. Then I spotted a music store across the street. Perfect.

I crossed my fingers as a little boost to my luck. "Luck be a needle tonight," I paraphrased the old song lyric. Then I crossed the street. Almost. Halfway across I got this: waa-waa, whoop-whoop, waaaa. A traffic cop on a motorcycle. I hadn't seen him or where he was hiding. A little obvious, I know, but I have to say that because I want you to believe me when I say I would not have jaywalked had I seen the policeman. I'm not that dense.

"Hey, you, come over here," he yelled at me. Not, of course, to the side of the street I was heading to but rather the side I had just left.

"You big ass," he counseled me. "You coulda been killed."

"I looked both ways," I said. (I hadn't.)

"Then you must be a blind son of a bitch."

"There were no cars," I defended myself. I had no idea if there were "no cars" or ten thousand cars. I was single-minded on getting to the music store. The needle, remember? Truth is I could have been passing through the Macy's Thanksgiving Day Parade and would have been oblivious to it.

"What do you call those?" He pointed to cars going in both directions. They were cars.

"Well," I said, "they weren't there before."

"Don't matter. You got any ID, a license?"

I almost lied and said, "No, I'm not driving today," but he had a look in his eye.

"Yeah, a driver's license." I handed it to him.

"Constantinople Ob? Is that your name?" I get this question a lot.

"Yes, it is."

"What kind of a name is that anyway?" This one, too.

"Oh, it's just my name."

"It's a funny one."

"No it isn't."

"It is if I say it is. You ought to change it." When I didn't say anything to his sarcasm, he went on. "So what do we do now? I caught you red-handed at jaywalking." It was an opening.

"Let me off with a stern warning?" My fingers, I noticed, were still crossed.

"That's very funny, just like your name, Mr. Ob."

"Ob."

"Huh, what?"

"Ob. My name is pronounced Ob. You pronounced it Ob."

"Do you think I care?"

"I just wanted you to know how it's pronounced," I told him. He did not seem to care, I noticed.

"Tell me something," he changed the subject, "just where were you going when you violated our pedestrian laws?" More sarcasm, that's for sure. I told him about my record player and the worn-out needle that needed replacing. "A record player, what are you, two hundred years old?" he asked me with more of that sarcasm. I said I like the old records and the pure sound you get from them.

"You are really a first-class numbnuts, aren't you?" He seemed to be having a testy day.

"No," I answered.

The officer was something of a multi-tasker, too, because throughout this whole confrontation he filled in the jaywalking ticket he handed me.

"Don't jaywalk, Mr. Ob, (wrong pronunciation, as you can tell) it's dangerous. And you have a nice day."

I crossed the street in the pedestrian zone and got to the music store where I was told they would have to order my needle as they did not keep them in stock. He said he would call me when it came in. When he asked my name and phone number, I had to go through that conversation about my name. That's getting old.

Down The Drain

There is something serious about home protection that needs to be brought to everyone's attention, and I am willing to describe it. I haven't seen anyone else address this issue and it only goes to show. Do I have to do everything, I ask.

Spiders. There it is, the topic sentence. I'll bet this gets your attention. Spiders. Not exactly the kind of house guests you get the spare bedroom ready for, are they? No, and I'll tell you why. They're spiders, that's why, the ones who crawl around your house and – saints preserve us – into your sock drawer and your shoes. Ugh.

I say there is a serious lack of understanding surrounding home protection. Then I say spiders. If I had a two-way camera, I am sure I would see most of you nodding in agreement. Studies show that the average homeowner – and research includes data from renters as well – has a bevy of tools and procedures to wage war against spiders. Some may say that "war is not the answer." To which I say, "Oh, yeah? They started it. They invaded our space without so much as a by-your-leave and set their sights on complete domination of our households."

And don't think that just because you see a single spider crawling up your bathroom wall that he or she is by himself or herself and is either lost or just out for his or her daily constitutional. That's exactly what they want you to think. The old bait and switch. No, not bait and switch, it's the old now-you-see-'em-now-you-don't. Maybe that's wrong, too. Regardless, it doesn't matter.

Those studies I mentioned tell us that the most popular response when encountering a spider inching along a bathroom wall is to secure it in the grasp of a facial tissue and then send it down the bathroom sink drain.

Fallacy!

Are you out of your mind? What have you done? How do you know that you haven't merely sent the multi-legged combatant right back to his or her fort? Have you ever been down that drain to learn what is there? Do you have a manual that includes this statement: "Don't bother looking into the drain for a spider encampment for you will not find one"? Of course you do not. No self-respecting plumbing contractor would try to get away with a statement like that. Or his lawyer.

Personally, I've lain awake many nights imagining a whole battalion of spiders trooping up out of my bathroom sink drain and making its way along porcelain and tiles to who knows what kind of mischief. It makes me very nervous. As a matter of fact, I can't go on with this even now.

Where You Got Those

A man of even temperament stood quietly on a street corner. When asked why he was standing in that particular place, he answered, "I am waiting for a bus." "Uh-huh, and why do you think that a bus will stop here so that you can get on?" "I did not say that I intended to get on the bus." "Ah-ha...right... yes...okay...that's true...you did keep that information to yourself. Perhaps I should have asked my question in a different manner." "Then again, perhaps you should refrain from poking your big, fat nose into other people's affairs."

The passerby – for it was a passerby who made the enquiry to the even-tempered man who had just gruffly betrayed his usual even-temperament with his uncharacteristic dismissal – passered on by.

Anon another pedestrian approached the even-tempered man, slowed down and edged in to say, "Hello." The hello was returned. The pedestrian said, "Nice day." "Indeed," replied the even-tempered man. The pedestrian then said, "I will wager five dollars with you that I can tell you where you got those shoes." The even-tempered man smiled. (He was from out of town.)

"Five dollars?" "Five dollars." "You will tell me where I got these shoes?" "I will tell you where you got those shoes." "Okay."

The pedestrian looked down at the shoes worn by the man of even temperament. He looked into the eyes of the man of even temperament. He looked up at the signpost above their heads and announced, "You got those shoes on your feet on the corner of Washington Boulevard and Lincoln Avenue." The two men stood at that very intersection. It was all true.

The even-tempered man, who could take a joke with the best of them, withdrew a five dollar bill from wherever it was he kept his folding money and handed it over to the pedestrian who thanked him and walked on. A bus rolled up to the intersection and stopped. It waited for the traffic light to change from red to green, then drove on. No one got on, no one got off.

Shortly, a policeman in his on-duty uniform walked toward the intersection. As he neared the man of even temperament, he saluted in a friendly manner raising his nightstick to the bill of his hat. The even-tempered man nodded back and said, "Do you have a moment, officer?" The officer did.

"I fear, sir, that there is nothing I can do about that," the officer said after the even-tempered man described how the pedestrian had used a clever ploy to secure a fin from him. "He did not commit a crime that I am familiar with." "I see your point," the man with the even temperament agreed, "though I am still short five dollars on the deal." "I fear so," the officer said, "and I wish I could offer more comfort." He seemed to enjoy using the word fear.

The even-tempered man thought for a moment then said, "I could be comforted if you gave me a chance to restore my five dollars." "Oh? How?" "I will give you five dollars if you can touch your elbow with your hand." As he spoke he gesticulated with his hand, bending his wrist toward his elbow. "But you will give me five dollars if you cannot and I can."

The policeman looked at the man of even-temperament and then surveyed the man's hand, wrist and elbow. "Are you double-jointed?" he asked. "Ask me no questions and I'll tell you no lies," the even-tempered man answered.

The policeman agreed to the challenge and was about to attempt the feat when he stopped suddenly and said sharply, "Hey, you aren't going to use your right hand and touch your left elbow are you?" "You are a man of keen observation I see. No, officer, I will not do that." Satisfied, the policeman then spent the next two or three minutes trying to touch his elbow with his hand. It was futile. He said, "I fear this is futile."

The even-tempered man said, "It is my turn then." Whereupon he reached with his right hand and touched the elbow of the policeman. He smiled warmly to the officer who by his look admitted defeat.

"Five dollars," the officer said. "Five dollars," said the man of even temperament. The man of even temperament reached out to collect the five dollars and make his financial dealings this day whole. Instead, the policeman rapped his nightstick across the fingers of the even-tempered man sending him into a paroxysm of agonizing pain and dancing about.

"Wow, does that ever hurt," the even-tempered man managed to say.

"Step aside," the policeman commanded, "unless you want more of the same. Well, do you?"

The man of even temperament stepped aside, not wanting more of the same.

Turkey Bowl

In the next sentence put the emphasis on the "I." Because it was a Saturday morning *I* won't forget soon. The day left several impressions on me.

Often on Saturday mornings I take walks in the neighborhood and almost as often through our local park. In the park on this Saturday I saw about a dozen fellows tossing around a football. I slowed to watch. While they were playing catch, one of them, a stocky figure, was taking charge to form teams. When he was finished arguing with one of the others he had two teams. One team was short by one player.

I had stopped some distance away watching all this.

"Excuse me," the stocky leader shouted at me. "You play football?" Do I play football? There's a good question. Yes, I play football. Played football. Not in about, well, for some years. Yet there are some skills you never lose.

"Yeah," I responded. "Come on over," he yelled. When I came on over I noticed that the other guys were younger than I, most were bigger, and most of them seemed to lack body fat.

"We need another player. Wanna play?"

"I haven't played in a few years."

"Oh, that's okay. We just play for fun. Nice and easy. Two hands below the waist. No tackling. Three over for a first down. Center's not eligible. Come on, it'll be fun. This is our annual Turkey Bowl. We've been doing this for about 10 years. One of the guys can't make it today. Something's up with his wife or something. My name's Dick, what's yours?"

"Constantinople Ob."

"Really? What kind of name is that anyway?"

"Oh, it's just my name."

"Okay. You're on their team. Over there. You're shirts." They play shirts and skins to tell the difference. It was a lovely November day, but I was still relieved I wasn't "skins."

The captain of my team told me to play center. "It'll give you a chance to see how we play." Seemed reasonable. In the huddle, the same guy called the play telling each fellow what to do. He talked authoritatively and confidently as if he had done this before. Me he told to block the guy coming in on two. At "two" nothing happened. "Hold on," he called. The guys on the other team laughed. "Snap the ball to me on two," he told me. "I'll go hut-hut and you snap it to me on the second hut."

"Okay," I said.

"Hut-hut," I heard. Then, "Oh, no." Unfortunately, the ball I snapped scraped along the ground to him and he had difficulty picking it up before the guy I was supposed to block got him two hands below the waist. I was lying on my back. "Nice and easy," as earlier described, was not how I saw things. These guys were serious.

I regrouped. Most of my snaps after that first one were successful. I even blocked that guy two or three times. That would account for the two or three bruises I had. I don't remember which play it was when I got the bloody lip.

We didn't score that first time we had the ball. On defense they told me to rush the passer. The game was almost all passes. Their center hiked the ball crisply and accurately to their passer and then he quickly shifted his feet into a classic blocking pose. He blocked me. Their passer had sufficient time to throw the ball successfully to his teammates.

Even when I moved farther and farther away from the center to start my pursuit of the passer he, the center, found a way to block me. He was awfully good. I don't want to accuse him of having a mean streak or anything, but on at least two occasions I think he intentionally used his knee to slow me down. As if I could go any slower after we had played for a short time. His knee caught me between the legs two times. Once before I got the bloody lip and once after.

When the score was 35-0 in favor of the team I was not on, I told the guys that I thought I had an appointment to get to and that I appreciated the invitation to join them in their annual event. I wished them all "Happy Thanksgiving." I would have shaken hands with them but my fingers were curled in so they wouldn't extend.

As I was walking away, I could feel the fruits of the game in my ankles, my shins, my knees, my groin, my ribs, my lungs, my shoulder and my lip. They, on their side, showed some courteous restraint until one of them called after me, "Nice game, Constantinople." That's when I heard the snickering.

130 Economists

I'll be the first to admit that I don't know anything about experimental psychology. So I was very surprised when I was asked to put 130 economists into a small room. I don't have 130 economists. I don't have them because I don't need them. What would I do with even a dozen economists?

As I think about it, a dozen economists could be a real boon. I could give them away as Christmas presents. "Merry Christmas, Uncle George, here's an economist." I haven't done any hefty reading into the matter, but it is more than likely that my gifts of economists to people on my Xmas list would almost assuredly be a first. Don't hold me to that, but I'm satisfied it would be. A first, that is.

Clearly, this poser had two obvious first steps. One, find 130 economists and, two, find a small room. But not necessarily in that order. Maybe finding the room first is more advisable because I'd want to be sure I had a place for 130 economists once they were rounded up. Absent a small room and I'd have nowhere to keep them while I was still room searching. They sure couldn't stay at my house. I have no space for 130 of anybody.

That was settled then. First, I'd look for a small room. Under "Rooms to Let" in the classified section of our town's newspaper I found several leads. And right from the beginning I had obstacles thrown in my pathway.

"How big are these economists you will be bringing to my room?" the first prospective landlady asked. I had no answer to give her except the very truthful "that's a good question." I've already explained that I do not have 130 economists. And you can correctly deduce that I do not have even one. Unless someone comes along who has inside information on the dimensions of economists and instructs me on the subject, I will remain in the dark.

All this I told another prospective landlady who, in time, said it really didn't matter to her just so long as the economists didn't smoke and didn't track mud into the rest of her house.

It was beginning to look like I was well on my way. I had located a small room, which, as I have said, was half the first part of the battle. I am nobody's fool. I knew that in an experiment such as this there could be many unforeseen turns of events that might easily spoil the whole affair.

So it was with a keen sense of attention to detail that I wrote down the address of the lady's house with the small room and made careful notes on how to get there by several different routes. She was very helpful with this. It would be egg on my face if I had 130 economists in my car and I didn't know how to get back to her house.

Right after that, however, is when she dropped the bombshell. Or so she thought. "Why," she queried, "are you going to put 130 economists into my small room?"

Because it was part of that psychology experiment about which I know nothing and could not explain or justify, I thought a moment and then announced, "Why not?" To that she had no answer.

Census

A Scotsman and a banjo player walk into a tavern in Inverness. They sit at the bar, leaving a stool empty between them. The Scot orders a stout, the musician a whisky sour. Each pushes money toward the barman who says, "You're not regulars. Where are you from?" The Scot says St. Andrews. The banjo player shrugs his shoulders. "Not talkative, eh?" the barman says to the Scot. "Dunno," the Scot answers after looking at the banjo player. "Maybe Nessie got his tongue," the barman says. "Who?" "Nessie." "Oh, maybe." The barman steps back and begins wiping glasses per his professional training.

A woman enters the tavern and looks around the pub before approaching the bar and taking the seat between the Scot and the banjo player. The barman edges closer and asks what he can get for her. She looks at the whisky sour and then at the stout. "Are you serving lunch?" she asks. "Yes, but only shepherd's pie and bangers and mash." "Then," she says, "I'll have an absinthe." At this the banjo player laughs and exclaims, "That was a wonderful non-sequitur." The barman says, "He does talk." The woman smiles at the barman and then nods at the banjo player. The Scot says nothing.

When a few minutes pass and no one has talked, the barman asks the Scot what he does for a living. The Scot says he is a furrier. "A furrier?" repeats the barman. "What does a furrier do?" The Scot answers, "A furrier supplies fur garments to women of taste." "Does he?" says the barman.

Turning to the banjo player, the barman asks him what he does for a living. "I am a banjo player," he reveals. "Interesting," the barman says, "can you make a living playing the banjo?" "Yes," the banjo player says. "Interesting," says the barman.

Not wishing to appear discriminatory, the barman says to the woman, "What do you do for a living?" "I am the director of the census for Scotland," she tells him. "Interesting," says the barman, "you count us, is that correct?" "Yes," the director says. "How many of us are there?" the barman asks. "More," she says, "than this room can hold." The barman smiles. So also do the Scot and the banjo player. Then the barman asks, "Are there more of us now than the last time you counted?" "I am glad you asked," the director of the census for Scotland replies, "for I can tell you." "Please do," the barman encourages her.

"As a Scotswoman from Perth I know of the worth," she smiles with mirth, "to say that about the girth of the Earth is no dearth of birth north of the Firth of Forth."

The ensemble says nothing for a moment as they digest the remark.

"Must be the cold weather," the banjo player offers. The barman laughs at the banjo player's little joke and says to the Scot, "Your friend is funny when he finally talks." The Scot says, "He is not my friend. I'm not unneighborly, you understand. I just don't know who he is."

The barman says, "Interesting."

Phone Message

Ring-ring, one. Ring-ring, two. Ring-ring, three. Ring-ring, four.

"Hello, this is…oh, wait, no. Here…hello, you have reached 555. Oh, shoot, area code first. Hello, you have reached 999-555-1492, extension…oh, shoot."

"Honey, what's our extension here? Do you know it? Honey. Honey!"

"What?"

"What's our extension here?"

"What?"

"Our extension, what is it?"

"What? I can't hear you."

"Put the baby down for a minute. She's probably yelling in your ear so you have a hard time hearing what I am saying."

"What?"

"Oh, balderdash. What…is…our…extension?"

"Just a minute. I'm going to put the baby down. She's been yelling in my ear so I have a hard time hearing what you are saying."

"I just want to know if you know our extension here. I'm recording our new telephone greeting and I need it."

"What? We have a phone call?"

"No, I am…oh, never mind about that. Is the baby down?"

"I put the baby down. What is it you want?"

"Our phone extension. What is it?"

"Phone extension? What are you talking about?"

"Our phone extension. I'm putting it in our greeting. What is it?"

"We don't have a phone extension. All we have is a phone number."

"Oh, yeah? What was I thinking?"

"You're asking me?"

"Well, I thought we had one. Never mind. I'll just go on."

"We are away from the phone right now and we cannot take your call. We will be back in..."

"Honey, when will we be back?"

"What?"

"For the phone greeting. When should I say we will be back?"

"Back from where?"

"From where we'll be when the phone rings."

"I'll probably be here with the baby."

"Sure, some of the time. But what about when we're out?"

"How long will we be gone?"

"That's what I want to know. I mean how long before we get back after we've gone out somewhere."

"Doesn't it depend?"

"What do you mean?"

"Won't it depend on how far away we are and when we start back?"

"Yes, I suppose so."

"And don't forget we won't be here to hear the phone ring. So it will also depend on that. You know, when the phone rings."

"This isn't as easy as I thought it would be."

"Say, have you got your recording on pause while we figure this out?"

"Oh, crud. This is going to be a long greeting."

"I'll bet. Just say we'll be back in thirty minutes."

"Okay."

Zanadu

The oldest man in the room at the Assisted Living Center said to read the Zanadu poem. He said it to me. I was a volunteer there reading stories and poems to the seniors in the recreation room.

I wish he hadn't asked for that one. It wasn't in the book of poems I was reading from. When he said to me to read it I went looking in the title index at the back of the book to find the page number. As I was looking, he said it again. "Read the Zanadu poem." I suspected he wanted that one because he said it a third time and again a fourth. I was at the Zs in the index, near the Zs is more like it because there was no poem shown under Z including Zanadu.

"Read the Zanadu poem," he repeated.

"I'm looking here, Tom, and I can't find it. I guess they didn't include that selection in this volume."

"Read the Zanadu poem."

"How about something nice from Robert Frost?" I offered.

"Did he write the Zanadu poem?" Tom wanted to know.

"I don't think so. Frost wrote, oh, here's a good one. How about 'Stopping by Woods'?"

"Is that the Zanadu poem?"

"Not really."

"*Whose woods these are...*" I started.

Tom asked, "Is this the Zanadu poem?"

"No, Tom, it's Frost's 'Stopping by Woods on a...' "

"Is that were Zanadu is? In those woods?"

"Well, no, not exactly. This is a different poem. You'll like it. Let me read it to you and to the others (almost all of whom were asleep in their chairs) and you'll see just how nice a poem it is."

"*Whose woods these...*"

"Is there trees in those woods?" Tom asked.

"Yes, I suppose there would be trees there since it is a woods Frost is writing about."

"*Whose woods these...*"

"Read the Zanadu poem."

"Sorry, Tom, I don't have that with me today. Tell you what, I'll look for it and bring it in next time. What say to that?" He said nothing.

"*Whose woods these...*"

"What is that?" Tom again.

"It's the poem by Frost. I'm sure you will enjoy it."

I tried again. "*Whose woods these are...*"

"Read the Zanadu poem."

"...I think I know..."

"I thought you were going to read to us about trees," Tom commented.

"Trees?"

"Yes, you said there were trees in Zanadu."

"No, what I said was..."

"Joyce Kilmer wrote 'Trees'," Tom said.

"Did she? Let me look in the index and see if it's in this book." Anything to get old Tom off his Zanadu kick. As I was flipping to the T's in the index, the dinner bell rang. The sleepers awoke and they, along with Tom, scurried to the dining hall. Scurried is a relative term as used here. I went home.

In A Train Station

I've told you in some of my Ob-servations that I have traveled some. It's true, and I think it is one of the attributes that helped me land the gig on *Word for Word*. Some of the other co-editors have not traveled, and Mr. Thom thought my travel experiences could bring a broader perspective to the writing of a dictionary and reference work.

Yes, I think you can learn a lot by going to a library all the time and sitting there reading books. What I ask though is what does that compare to actually experiencing other places. Sorry, it should be "how" does that compare. Well, it doesn't.

Take, for example, an encounter I had with a young woman outside a train terminal in Paris. I was there once. She came up to me and asked for some money. Poor thing, I thought, and she looked so sweet. I put down my suitcases and took out a few euros and gave them to her.

You may not agree with my point of view, but I am a fan of the euro. You can go from country to country and not have to go through the hassles of the converting-your-money thing like the old days. Before, you had to go to a *wechsel* here, a *bureau de change* there and all the while you're paying a fee to get different money. And then you have to start all over trying to figure out what the money means. The euro is a good answer for that.

Oh, the young lady in Paris. I gave her the money and watched as she trotted away. Then I reached down to get my luggage only to discover they'd been stolen. You won't find that kind of travel experience reading a book in a library.

Well, you will now because it's in here.

When I travel I like to mix with the people. Not con artists in Paris train stations, I can assure you. Despite that bad experience, it's who I am. I just think you get more out of travel by interacting. Be sure to get a good handle on local customs, however, and take note of travel cautions before you go since any shortage of that knowledge can come back to bite you, which means there could be "funny" things that will happen. But not how funny my friends thought it was when I told them about my incident at the Paris train station and that French slut and her thieving friends.

Sit For A Spell

You just never know, do you? Someone says one thing and something happens that you don't expect. You're out on the highway and you're trying to get a ride at night and a car stops and you get in and the guy says, "Where ya headin," and you tell him and he says, "I'm headin that way, too," and he starts out and you end up in a slash and gash horror flick at the losers end of the slashing and gashing. You just never know, do you?

Or you're driving down a back road and you lose your bearings and you stop at a farmhouse and the owner says, "What's doin," and you say you've lost your bearings and he says he thinks he can help and you say thanks. Then he says it. He says, "Come on in and sit for a spell." You're in and you're sitting when he says, "What'll ya have?"

"Humm?" you murmur.

"Lemonade or apple cider?"

"Oh," you say, and choose between the two.

"Okay," he says, "ennui."

"Excuse me?"

"Ennui."

"What about it?"

"Ennui, how do you spell it?"

"Oh, sorry, didn't understand. You know what, I don't know how."

"Okay, it's e-n-n-u-i."

"Oh."

"Predilection."

"I beg your pardon?"

"Predilection, how do you spell it?"

"I'm not sure. Should we look it up in the dictionary?"

"No, that would be cheating."

"It would?"

"Sure. Predilection. P-r-e-d-i-l-e-c-t-i-o-n."

"Oh, never heard that before."

"Tertiary."

"What?"

"Tertiary."

"Pardon me, but what is going on here?"

"A spell."

"A spell? What do you mean?"

"I don't mean anything. Earlier, I asked you to come in and sit for a spell. This is the spell."

"Ha, ha, ha. I thought you meant something altogether different. I thought you meant to sit for a time. You know, sit for a spell."

"That doesn't make any sense at all, sit for a time. I got a watch of my own and it keeps good time. I look at it if I need to know the time."

"Well, thank you for the drink, lemonade, wasn't it?"

"No, it was the cider."

"Oh, yeah, cider, thanks. I best be going."

"Where are you heading?" the farmer asks.

"East."

"But you said you lost your bearings."

"Well, yeah, uh-huh, but I'll be going just the same."

"At night, in the dark, on back roads, lacking your bearings? Come on out back and I'll get a map."

"Good, thanks."

"Don't mind the smell. We've been chuckin chickens today."

"Chuckin chickens?"

"Yeah."

"What does that mean?"

"Getting them ready."

"Getting them ready for what?"

"For eating, of course. Come on, I'll show you."

"Well, I really need to be getting on my way."

"Nonsense. This will take just a minute. Right in here. Here's where we chuck our chickens. Don't mind the smell, there's a little blood. Zebadiah, he doesn't call it chuckin chickens. He says we slash and gash. Zebadiah, he's our youngest. He goes to a lot of movies. That's what he calls them, slash and gash flicks. Did you ever? We don't know what he'll come up with next. Zebadiah."

"You keep your maps out here?"

"Maps? No. Oh, yeah, my maps. Out here. Yeah. Come on to the back room with me and I'll get out my, uh, maps. Don't mind the smell. Where'd you say you thought you were headin again?"

The "Off the Grid" Interlude

The Announcement

(John Thom writes:)

Before we get to "The Announcement," let me just say that we can't hold it against him, but while C. Ob was "ob-serving" life and morals and culture and world developments that turned into the "Ob-servations" in his blog, he determined that a titanic change in lifestyle was irresistible. He moved "off the grid." Like other best-selling authors who have done the same, Ob removed himself from conventional society, ridding himself of all the trappings of an everyday citizen. The following Ob-servations and other reports in this Interlude section are from his blog during that period in his life. Keep that in mind while you are studying these. Now the announcement:

I have some very startling news about my colleague, Constantinople Ob. You know him for his famous "Ob-servations" and his valued contributions to *Word for Word*, the dictionary everyone is talking about, or they would be if some publisher would see the error of its way and do the right thing.

I must confess that the news hit me more with shock than with surprise. I didn't anticipate it, but as it sank in I could look back and say, "I should have seen something like this coming."

All of the co-editors of *Word for Word* have special creative and academic qualities. The eclecticism of the co-editors is one of the reasons the dictionary is so potent. I subjected each co-editor to a penetrating pre-selection interview. During these I uncovered what made each of them such compelling personalities in addition to their capabilities as philologers.

With Mr. Ob the interviewing was especially interesting. His *curriculum vitae* spoke for itself, but Mr. Ob himself, that was different. He was, shall we say, guarded about some portions of his past. He shared his more obvious history and job progressions, but he tended to shield his personal relationships, not that that would have been a mark against him. There were, a background report revealed, no felonies, for example. He was not hiding a dark past.

So while it is shocking to hear his news, it is not surprising. The news is not an opening into a dark past, it is rather a dark future he is entering.

Constantinople Ob has elected to live "off the grid." Like the now infamous John Twelve Hawks, who wrote a New York Times best-selling novel, Mr. Ob is going underground. In a final meeting with me, he explained that he has had growing concerns for quite a while about the intrusiveness by governmental and public institutions and other authoritarian organizations into all of our lives.

"I plan to cut ties to everyone and everything," he told me. "I will rid myself of all the baggage of a middle class scholar, except for my favorite books. I will move to a new location. I will stop driving, cutting my driver's license to shreds and cancelling my auto insurance. I will go to an all-cash payment system. I will..."

He went on in some detail as to how he would conduct himself out of the prospect of those who he felt wanted to delve uninvited into his affairs. "Who are they?" I asked. "It just goes to show," he answered, "your naiveté that you even ask the question." "That's quite non-responsive," I challenged him. He looked at me in a most suspicious way.

Anyway, he said he would continue to write and dictate his Ob-servations. I was relieved to hear that. I asked him how I was to pay him for these contributions. He said he was opening a numbered account in a bank in a brand new country comprising three small islands in the South Seas. "They told me they have staff known for their discretion," he said.

"Where will you live?" I asked him. "Well of course I can't tell you that," he said. "Living off the grid means not revealing where one lives. I can tell you, though, that it'll be within a bicycle ride to a great little Mexican diner I know."

I'm sure he means Tito's Tacos out west in Culver City, California. To me that shows good judgment.

Substitute Blog Manager

(John Thom writes:)
When Constantinople Ob went "off the grid" he left a bit of a vacuum in the management of this blog. I should have mentioned this to you earlier, but it escaped my attention in the wake of the devastating news of his dramatic

change in lifestyle. My schedule does not permit me to spend endless hours in front of a computer screen and keyboard to make sure the blog is pertinent and up-to-date. Therefore, I have enlisted another of the co-editors of *Word for Word* to take on that important role. (I asked Dr. Ives, out of courtesy for his longevity and his sometime usefulness to the dictionary, but I did not hear back from him.) My other choice, and please do not assume this is a second choice, is Barbara "Babs" Buhl-Buhl. She gladly accepted. I'm sure her occasional lapses in memory will not interfere with her dedication to serving my interests and yours, the readers. Thank you.

Off The Grid

This is my first Ob-servation since I informed Mr. T. of my decision to live "off the grid." In it I will go over some of the steps I needed to take to sever all connections to where I just was and who I just was.

You may wonder why I have chosen to go underground. There are many reasons. Some will be those you will recognize. Others will, perhaps, open your eyes to a new understanding in your own lives. I think, however, that I need to collect my thoughts so that the Ob-servation that details the sizable decision I've made will be the telling testament that it deserves to be.

In the meantime, I'll wager you all have heard the old homily that we don't own our possessions, they own us. This is never more true than when you move. You discover things you forgot you had; you don't have enough boxes (and you annoy your friends and neighbors asking them for theirs); you agonize over which items to keep and which to dispose of; and you weigh the pluses and minuses of holding a yard sale.

This is exactly where I was as my move date approached. So I bit the bullet and posted signs on light poles around my neighborhood announcing a yard sale on Saturday morning. I had not ever held one of these events before. I thought it would be in competition with other households moving out of the neighborhood. So I was a little surprised, but delighted, to discover there were no other yard sale flyers posted for the same Saturday as mine.

Starting about 6 a.m. I put loads of things out along my driveway and front yard. There was clothing, pictures, furniture, record albums, glassware and other dishes, garden tools…you name it. Well, don't name books. Those I am keeping.

It wasn't easy. About 6:30 a.m. people were arriving to look over my stuff. It was really unnerving to answer their questions while I was lugging things from inside to outside. My announcement was perfectly clear. It said the sale would begin at 8 a.m. Not 6:30. Can't people read?

The hardest thing, though, is how to put a price on things. You want to get rid of everything. I mean that's the whole idea of a yard sale, isn't it? But then you wonder if your price is too high or too low. Turns out that the price has little meaning. Everyone thinks they're in some foreign country where haggling is a constitutional imperative.

Anyway, it got to be eight o'clock and there was a nice little crowd there. People were looking over my stuff even as they were looking over their shoulders up and down the street. Surprisingly, none of my neighbors came over. Some of them were watching from their porches.

It was shortly after eight-thirty when a police car rolled down the street. Some of the shoppers in my yard noticed and scurried away to their cars. I was curious about that. The police stopped in front of my yard and tooted that little horn-like thing they have in their cars. I looked up and waved at them. The rest of the shoppers headed toward their cars. I was curious again. Now the police hit their siren a quick one-two. Woo-woo. I waved again.

"Get over here," the policeman driving the car yelled at me.

"What?" I asked when I got next to the driver-side door.

"What are you doing?" the officer asked me as if he didn't already know the answer.

"What do you mean?" I said.

"Just what are you doing here," he said, a little pointedly.

"I'm selling my stuff. I'm moving."

"You can't do that," he told me.

"I can't move?"

"No, you can't sell your stuff."

"I don't want it anymore. I'm changing my lifestyle," I said to him masking my real intentions about going off the grid. I was sure he wouldn't understand that. Moreover, he would likely make a note of it in my file somewhere.

"I don't give a shit where you're going or what you're going to do. You just can't sell your stuff here."

"Why?"

"Because it's against the law." At this point my anxieties about the pervasiveness of the oppressive authoritarian construct in our lives put me on edge.

"Against the law? What law?"

"It's a city ordinance. Yard sales are not permitted."

"I didn't know that."

"You do now. So put your dumb shit away and don't do it again."

I had no answer. When I didn't say anything the cop looked at me and said, "We're going to come back by here in fifteen minutes and we better not see any signs of a yard sale. Do you get me?" I nodded. I had everything put away in about twenty minutes. Those cops never did come by again.

For Your Information

(Babs Buhl-Buhl writes:)

Before Constantinople Ob moved off the griddle to take his place undetectable underground, he completed two Observations. I was asked to review them when John Thom invited me to manage the blog. This I did. I was preparing to post them in the blog before he held his revealing meeting with John, er Mr. Thom. Owing to the nature of his decision and subsequent announcement, I determined it would be best to delay posting. This I did. Now that the news is filtering throughout the blog community and Mr. Ob is known to have separated from our more conventional orbits, I re-evaluated his previously written blogs to see if it was time to post them. This I did. Below is the first one. The second will follow in a timely manner. Your comments, I guess, are solicited.

Mustaches

I suppose every youth has looked in a mirror only to remark, "I'd look pretty awesome with a mustache." And that's when it begins. A few days without shaving the upper lip, searching the bathroom for a comb of just the right size and shape to be on hand when the hairs start to resemble those of someone you admire for dash and élan, asking your friends if they can see any evidence yet, constantly stroking your lip in hopes of that telling first growth of bristles.

It should be understood that your genetic imprint is likely to have a great deal to say about the development of your mustache. Parental and grandparental genes are going to help determine several factors: rate of growth; color; curliness; coarseness; etc.

See? Most kids just don't think like that. No, they say "I want a mustache" on Monday and fully expect to look like Errol Flynn on…no, it was Clark Gable…on Saturday.

Remember I said it was genetics that would have a great deal to say about the relative success of your mustache-growing adventure? Some of you are going to be disappointed because you come from families with fair skin and a real paucity of hair or a lot of blondes in the family tree. And you know what that means. If you don't, let me inform you. It means you will have much less success in growing a mustache that others will remark on and one that does not embarrass you.

I know that what I have just said may hurt, cut to the quick as they say, but it had to be said. If you learn anything from my bluntness, that's good. Some of you, however, may be tempted to try something different. This I advise against. Now you know where I stand on that.

Oh, what is it? Let me tell you. It's that temptation to get your mom's mascara pencil and augment your otherwise colorless coloration. This takes you on a real slippery slope. You start with a little outline just under the nose, move to a drooping along the edges of the mouth, and then the coup d'etat (coup de grace?) of the chin whiskers to complete the classic goatee. The really foolhardy next step is also often taken and that's the addition of longish sideburns. By this time you are already looking for another mascara pencil. You didn't heed the cautions.

If it's one thing I have learned about mustaches it's that men tend to have more success with these than women.

(Rebuttal to "Mustaches" by Babs Buhl-Buhl:)
Will this never end? Will the sharp-tongued and miserable little men out there ever stop to think how their supposedly funny jokes hurt others? I know how it hurts. Yes, you may laugh when your buddies or pals talk about a woman's appearance. You call it locker room humor. All the guys together swapping their ribald stories with no one courageous enough to speak up and say, "This is not right."

Okay, some women have to take steps to control unwanted hair on some places on their bodies. We...women, that is, have both medical avenues and personal care products as answers. We...they don't ask to have this need, no, they are victims. Victims don't need more of the off-hand ridicule found in this so-called "Ob-servation." They need understanding.

Where understanding is not found is in the likes of this Limerick I forced the others to withhold from the definition of "mustache" in *Word for Word*. Then I said to myself that it would serve as a good lesson to publish it here where I could demonstrate how men can sting the feelings of women. It is decidedly not funny. Here it is:

A woman whose secret she wouldn't share
This she kept safe in her private lair.
The secret she guarded
Was one she regarded
As too little lip under her hair.

Bird Bath

This will be a very short Ob-servation because I am in a hurry. I don't like to be rushed by things. I never have because it seems like I am not using my time effectively. But now that I am off the grid, I have to conduct myself differently.

There's something else, too. I've been getting messages from Ms. Buhl-Buhl that my contributions should arrive earlier so that she can edit them and then schedule them for posting. I can't argue with her. No, not because I disagree with her. It's that I'm off the grid and we aren't in direct contact. If you're wondering how I get messages from her, I can't reveal that either. That's what living off...oh, you know.

And this business of her editing my Ob-servations is causing me some discomfort. Perhaps by mentioning it here she will remember just who the author of these Ob-servations is and will desist from making any unnecessary changes. (I do have to admit that I am not the sharpest speller. Ha-ha-ha.)

Okay, my Ob-servation. This episode happened a while back. I mentioned recently, I think, that I owned a BB gun. No, wait, that comes later.

What happened was I used to have a bird bath in my garden. Not now, of course, because I don't have a garden now, but I used to. I didn't keep water in...do you even know what I'm talking about? Maybe you haven't seen a bird bath. It's a kind of heavy structure usually made out of cement or plaster or something heavy like that so it won't tip over. It's got a base and then a top where the water goes so birds can drink. I guess they could take baths in it, too, if they wanted. Why else would it be called a bird "bath"? You have to wonder, however, whether it's sanitary to bathe and drink in the same place. I do.

I didn't keep water in it because the birds tended to gather in big crowds and make a lot of noise, chirping and all. Don't misunderstand me, I like birds, most of them anyway, but before, when I did keep water in the bird bath, they'd collect there and set up a real racket.

What the devil! When I said "I do" I didn't mean that I bathed and drank from the same water. Oh no. I meant that I wonder whether when birds do that if it's really sanitary. For them.

Back to the birds. I like the way birds sing and all, but when a whole crowd of them comes together it can be a real cacophonous event. (Like that? Cacophonous?)

So I stopped putting water in it. A few birds kept coming back to, I guess, see if there was any water. There wasn't. Must have been the dumber birds. Maybe it was because they're smarter than I thought and they were trying to antagonize me, but those black and gray and white ones would show up and squawk like crazy at all times of the day and night. I think they're called mockingbirds. What a perfect name.

Now I have to tell you about the BB gun. (Do you suppose they're called bb guns instead of BB guns? I really don't know.) Things reached a point where I thought I'd have to do something about the loud birds. So I got the BB gun out (I'm going to stick with BB and not bb) and I would shoot at them. Not to hit them really, but to scare them off.

Trouble was, I'd do that and it would work for a while and then they'd come back. I'd get so mad that I'd think about, oh, what the heck, I admit it, I'd think about actually shooting them. I'd think it's no big deal to kill a mockingbird.

(Babs Buhl-Buhl writes:)
I haven't changed anything in this guy's writing that wasn't very helpful. And his suggestions about how I play my role, he can just stop that griping right now. And this one, his latest Observation, only goes to show something about him. It breaks my heart. It is just mean. Shooting birds with a beebee gun? How awful.

The Fair Sex

In my observations until now I think I've been remiss by neglecting a subject that gets too little attention in the popular media where people get most of their news and opinions. That's the plight of women in our society. It's like politics and religion, topics we tend to skirt because they are charged with so much emotion, topics, too, that people say you can't change other people's minds, so why bother.

Bother? What's so terrible about trying to correct all the ills that befall women because they are viewed as the "weaker sex" only because they can't lift a 100-lb barbell over our heads? Why not bother, I (Constantinople Ob) say, when corrective action could mean so much to half our population?

Now that I am living off the griddle I can see from a new vantage point just how much harm is caused to women by men. Not all men, maybe, but many who still think that their, or our, buddy-buddy, towel-snapping, macho attempts at humor are just base inaccuracies and misogynistic venom that only hurts women.

We see women trapped in stereotypical roles and we do nothing about it. Why can't women be doctors or lawyers or senators or astronauts like men? They are not just waitresses, hair stylists, nurses or actresses.

Statistics show that more than half of the population of our country are women. But do women represent half of the influential institutions that play an integral part in our lives? No, they don't. I, for one, find that unacceptable.

Look, too, at the earnings record of women. They earn less than men.

I believe the worst expression of the way men put down women is the way they are treated as sex objects. No matter what a woman does in public she is categorized sexually. You wouldn't categorize your mother in this manner, so why do you do it when it is someone else? The answer is you see them as the butt of jokes or as just common playthings. Let me ask you this, do you ever hear of a man being called an airhead or a bimbo? No.

I've been off the griddle for several weeks and I have been out of touch with some of the news, but I did see one telecast about that up-and-coming actress who was subjected to so much unfortunate publicity. Her face was all over the news that night. Tears and everything. If she had been a man she would have stood a better chance to avoid the intense and unjustified attention. Just because she is of the female gender, she is portrayed as a sex object by the hordes of newspapers and televisions and internets.

I would like to say that these views about women must change. I would like to say also that I know how it can be done. But I can't. I am a man. I don't have the answer.

Perils

I'm no hero. Even though I had loads of e-mails reach my old computer address and tweets congratulating me on my choice of a new lifestyle, I cannot claim any sort of victory. The change is dictated by necessity, by the tenor of the times.

Take just one example. Where I lived before moving, our community was served by a natural gas distributing company. Our apartments, homes and offices used this resource for heating and cooking. A competing company also served customers but with electric, not gas, power.

That said, what possible reason was there for our local councilperson to hold a public forum innocuously titled "Energy in the 21st Century." Get this, if you attended the meeting, you had to sign an attendance sheet with your name, address, phone number, e-mail address, twitter account, blog name (if applicable) and your energy company (gas or electric.) I faked all of them.

Every step of the way nowadays the authorities governing our lives are collecting information from us. It is left to me to ask, "Towards what end?" Yes, it is a good question. Furthermore, why does your grocery store insist you put in your telephone number to effect a simple "store club" discount? I won't do it. I just pay full fare for my groceries. Of course, I don't have a phone anymore. Others will have to consider this question as well as its implications. Your grocer, think about it.

Sure, I've given up many parts of my past. It is the path you must take to go underground, to live off the grid. Some have been hard. Hard to give up, that is. I'll name a few. Magazine subscriptions. That ought to be obvious because it pits their information about you and your interests combined with the postal system putting a carrier at your front door every day (what's with that!) against your waning power to resist.

I also gave up my membership in one of those "big box" stores. I always felt I benefited in the long run by buying certain items in bulk, but once again it was a matter of severing ties. One last example of the parts of my past that needed shedding is my passport. What more revealing document could there be for them to know not only who you are, but also where you are or have been or where you are going?

No one has accused me of it yet, though I suspect it would not be long before someone does, so I'll just raise it now to stave off any useless debate. I am not paranoid; just look at the evidence.

(Babs Buhl-Buhl writes:)
This next one is just unbelievable. Can you believe what he's done now? Just look at this.

Modern

You can say what you will about my upbringing, like I didn't have strong parental controls, like teachers spent more time with the "quicker" students, that I had nightmares, that I was a perennial bed wetter, oh, I mean bench-warmer. Along the way, however, I did some okay things, too.

One I'm very proud of. I learned early to be considerate about others, and so it should come as no surprise to anyone reading this that I do not support woman suffrage. For years we've heard about this and nowhere have I seen any actions or programs implemented to strike a blow for the ladies. It is not confined to just America either. You hear about this from other countries as well. Why is it so widespread? This is the modern age for crying out loud. Can't we get past this?

The suffrage. More precisely, women's suffrage. Let's look it up together right now and see whether there is a possible remedy for the suffering in the word itself. Suffrage: "The right to vote." Why are women and not men so afflicted? Why...wha..."right to vote"? I thought it meant something else. Honest. Doesn't it *sound* like suffering? It did to me. Well, live and learn.

How about that. Where do I go from here? This looks like a dead-end now, and I have all this space left. I could just drum my fingers on the desk-top and fade away. But no. While I've got your attention, let's look at something else. In fact, it's up a little toward the front of this Ob-servation and it is a subject that I was considering for a future essay.

A few minutes back I made reference to the "modern age." Have you ever wondered about that? Like when did it begin? I have and I'll wager, yes, you have also.

The "modern age." That's the one we're in now judging from the name. Modern means (and this time I'll look it up before I proceed very far into this discussion) "recently or the present." Whew, I was right.

We have a fairly good handle on other ages and when they were. What good's your encyclopedia set if you can't go in there and get the birthdates of the Ice Age, the Iron Age, the Jazz Age, for example?

Here's the problem, though. No one, it appears, has yet to try to pin down the start of the "modern age." No one until now. I am prepared to go out on a limb a short way and proclaim it. The start date. Sorry, at least the start *year.* The day itself may be a tad challenging.

So here it is. It was 1927. Maybe 1903. I don't know which company it was or which model of car, but it was certainly the introduction of the windshield wiper on automobiles. That stroke of mechanical genius easily catapulted us from a pre-modern age to a modern age. 1927. Maybe 1903.

I just wish we had the name of the man who dreamed it up. How it came about is not hard to fathom. A rainy day, a drive in the country, hanging his head out of the side screen to see his way. And bingo! Wipe the water from the "windscreen." It already met that goal, i.e., holding the "wind" from the faces of the occupants of the car. Why not the rain, too? 1927. Maybe 1903.

Say, I am sorry about that woman suffrage misunderstanding a while ago. I hope something like that doesn't happen again.

A Gut-Piercing Revelation

(John Thom writes:)

This post is not from Constantinople Ob, who is off the grid, not off the "griddle," nor is it from our erstwhile blog manager, Babs Buhl-Buhl. It is from me. I want that clear. It is a painful message to deliver to our readers. You have all shown wonderful loyalty along with a steely attentiveness to C. Ob's Ob-servations, so to admit in this posting that you have been buffaloed shakes my resolve to the core.

I was at my wit's end when I was finally tracked down on a trip out of town. I was busy enough to have missed a few days of blog postings here. Yes, at my wit's end, so much so that I considered abandoning the whole affair. Shutting down the blog. But close friends convinced me otherwise by reminding me of the faith you readers have put into Constantinople's Ob-servations. There is the rub. A recent Ob-servation, one in which you were lectured on the merits of women (a point no one in our venture here or on the staff of *Word for Word* will gainsay) was not written by C. Ob. It was entitled, "The Fair Sex."

I hope you can recover from this. It has been very hard for me. I can only speculate how Mr. Ob himself will take this when it becomes apparent to him. But as he is off the grid there is no way to learn his true feelings until he is ready to share those with us. Perhaps at a later time.

The explanation of this travesty is contained in the following letter of resignation. I print it verbatim although I considered against that. The vitriol in it exceeds the limits usually associated with responsible American publishing. It does, however, open a window into this sordid affair, so you should read it uncensored.

I, Barbara Buhl-Buhl, being of sound mind and aware of my actions, took an unusual approach to my new job recently when I, of my own volition, prepared and posted a draft under the impression it was by Constantinople Ob. He did not write it. I did.

That crazy son-of-a-bitch couldn't have expressed the needs of women if he had been born one. All he does is look at the little things of life. Dogs and cats and cribbage and state maps and…oh, hell, you've read these mindless ramblings so you know what I mean.

I'm sure he's also the asshole who put all those wisecracks in Word for Word *about women. He thinks I don't know that, but he "dated" Raquel Jones, one of the co-editors of* Word for Word, *a few times when we were drafting* Word for Word *and she confided in me a few things that would support my assertions if I were someone to speak "out of school." I can tell you that Raquel told me C. Ob has an "uncommon" interest in the dating scene. You can draw your own conclusions about that.*

And where is the little prick? "Off the grid?" What does that mean? What a dickhead he is. I'll tell you right now that no one I know misses the putz. He's probably just hiding from the law or from the IRS or from a wife and family. I hope he's hiding from the mob! They never quit looking.

I'll tell you something else. It won't be long before he's back. One thing I remember was how helpless he is. Some of the girls on the co-editor staff and I used to joke about him. Mary

Martha said Ob couldn't make a grilled cheese sandwich without attending a two-week seminar on the procedure.

Well, I resign as blog manager. Big friggin deal. What's a blog anyway? A place to show how stupid you are, or that you don't have a clue how to express yourself even in your own language. I hope Ob is run over by a truck.

Personal Statement From C. Ob

I am going to have to choose my words very carefully as I write this Ob-servation. I want it to say exactly how I feel and, at the same time, reflect the usual control over any emotional content in my views. Simply put, I don't want to "lose it." No one, however, would fault me, I trust, if I did, as the reason for this particular Ob-servation is very personal.

I don't like to insert myself into these Ob-servations except as I might be the eyes and ears objectively chronicling human behavior in all its many and varied forms. I could be any other person taking note of the subjects addressed in this series. But when a turn of events occurs and it involves me directly (and personally), then I need to change gears and ask for your forbearance in an Ob-servation that may, nay, will be cloaked in unfamiliar clothes.

As you are aware, I am living off the grid. One of the sacrifices here is a limitation on the access to conventional media. I sometimes don't see the news as it is being reported the first time around. Likewise, I do not enter the world wide web environment every day. It is for this reason that I did not see the "Ob-servation" entitled "The Fair Sex" until some time after it was posted. Can you imagine my surprise? Can you imagine my dismay? Can you imagine, ultimately, my growing anger? I don't know. You see, I did not write that Ob-servation. I assume you know that now.

Imagine, too, John Thom. His dismay. I am so grateful that he leaped so quickly and decisively when he uncovered the deceit that woman tried to perpetrate. He fired her right on the spot. Being the big-hearted guy he is, he let her write a letter of "resignation." Did you read it? You should. It just goes to show you.

The lies that are in it. I didn't "date" Raquel Jones. We are just good friends, and it hurts to see those things Raquel may have said about me, that is, if you can believe that Buhl-Buhl woman. "Babs" always was a mercenary type of character. Some women are known to have a heart of gold. You know the ones. She, on the other hand, has a heart of thirty pieces of silver.

I just don't believe that she could misuse the trust Mr. Thom put in her and then how she could deceive you as readers of this blog. I have to face the facts, I guess. Do you think that she thought this blog was a collaborative effort? I don't know. Am I being too easy on her? I don't know that either. Maybe I'm not getting enough protein. Anyway, it is back to business.

Celebrating

You might wonder what it is really like to live off the grid when you consider it is a 24-hour-a-day, seven-days-a-week, 4.3-weeks-a-month, 12-months-a-year chore.

I don't want to bore you with "a day in the life under ground," only I suspect you may want some insight into the issues I and others face. Any number of you readers may even now be considering the lifestyle change I made. I know how tempting it is vis-à-vis the existential threats to our privacy we all encounter daily.

Threats, yes, and none could be more unwanted than to be found out, i.e., to bump into somebody from your past. That would mean you'd need to do a lot of explaining. Hold on. There is one other threat that is probably more threatening (does that make sense?) and it is to be apprehended by someone who is out to get you.

But let's move on before I run out of time on this dictating machine. Where I am now, the local Chamber of Commerce puts on an Independence Day parade. It's a delightful presentation of local churches, schools, dance clubs, antique auto enthusiasts, horses, you name it. Don't name floats; it's not that kind of big-budget parade.

I went. I had on a non-descript pair of Bermuda shorts, a faded blue polo shirt, two layers of sunscreen, a broad-brimmed hat and sunglasses. And sneakers. I was assured of the anonymity that I have treasured for myself. It worked.

Up until the moment I heard exclaimed from a little distance away, "Well did you ever! That's you, isn't it, Ob?" Caught unawares, I looked over. Others as well did the same because the greeting, if you want to call it that, was heard by everybody in the vicinity.

So I got up slowly and began walking away. "Ob," the cry persisted, "you can run but you can't hide." I wasn't running. By now, also, I recognized the voice. It was that twerp from my old neighborhood. The same yahoo who said he'd be block captain for our Neighborhood Watch and then didn't do the first thing about it. What the deuce was he doing here? Whereas I didn't want to encounter anyone from my past, the fact is I didn't want to see this monkey under any circumstances. "Hey, Ob, hold on a minute!" he yelled again.

I stopped. He approached, laughing. "Hey, whater ya doin here?" he asked. (I was at a parade. What did he expect me to say?) "Wherer ya livin now?" he asked. (I told him I was living in London.) "Whater ya doin there, that's a long way away, ininit it?" he asked. (I told him I was now a member of the British Parliament.) "No kiddin," he said. (The guy is about as dim as a spent campfire.) I told him I had to catch a plane to England and walked away.

Later that day I indulged myself in a passion I've had since my childhood, but one I hadn't enjoyed in some years. I bought a package of fireworks I'd seen for sale on a highway into my town. Sorry, I can't tell you where. My town, that is, not where the fireworks stand was.

Like I say, I indulged myself. I waited until dusk and brought the fireworks out. I lit a "fleur de lis" in the middle of the street and it sent up a stream of pretty colors. Then another one. A few people came out to watch. Then more. I handed sparklers to the children and lit them (the sparklers) but not before telling them (the children) to be very careful with them (the sparklers) and not to throw them (the sparklers; it's not easy to throw children.)

I had a nice crowd out watching now and I felt good. It was fun to hear them "oohing and aahing" then applauding each little display of colorful eruptions. I had saved several bigger displays for some kind of grand finale.

When I walked out and lit one of these and watched it send up a wonderful array, I was surprised to hear no reaction.

I turned around and saw that everyone was going home, sort of fast. What the…had I insulted anyone? That's when I heard the familiar "pronk-pronk" of the horn-like gadget in police cars. I had heard it before. I turned around the other way and sure enough there was a police car.

"Come here," the policeman driving the car yelled over to me.

"What?" I said.

"Just what do you think you're doing?"

"You know, a little 4th of July fun. It's traditional."

"Well, stop it."

"Huh?"

"Didn't you hear…" He hesitated. "Say, don't I recognize you?"

"Me?"

"Yeah, you're the numnuts who tried to hold a yard sale. Do you go around looking for ways to make trouble?"

"What do you mean?"

"You know what I mean." I didn't and I said so. "You can't do fireworks here," he said.

"Oh, you mean not in the street. Should I move them to the sidewalk?"

"Are trying to piss me off?" I wasn't and I said so.

"Maybe we ought to run his ass in," the policeman said to the other officer in the car. The other officer looked at me and didn't say anything. He didn't seem to be too interested in me or the fireworks. But then I heard the other office say, "You're armed, why don't you shoot him?" They both laughed. Then the first officer said, "Get this crap out of here now, or I'll arrest you."

"But why?"

"Because it's against the law. Fireworks are not permitted in this city." I did not know that and I said so.

"You must be the most ignorant person I've ever run across," he said to me. That may be true about certain city ordinances, but he really didn't have to take that tone.

New Blog Manager

(John Thom writes:)

It's not as if I could just put an ad in the "Help Wanted" columns of the papers or post a 3x5 card in the unemployment office "seeking a blog manager," but what choice did I have? Ms. Buhl-Buhl proved to be a big disappointment.

Ms. Buhl-Buhl's departure meant I had to retain someone new since I cannot do the job myself. Nothing along those lines has changed. My work schedule will not unleash near enough time to allow that. Thus the ad. Yes, you are right that I could have looked again at the posse of co-editors of *Word for Word*. I did consider that for a short time, but the idea of an outsider, someone not exposed too closely to the pitiful actions of Ms. Buhl-Buhl... that appealed to me.

The ad ran and I got a couple of phone calls. The first was from Constantinople Ob's nephew, the one Con has written of. He tried to pass himself off as somewhat older than he actually is and with more education and experience. I can see now why Con has been less than complimentary of this young rapscallion. While he was trying to trick me into hiring him I could hear his friends in the background making dirty remarks and imitating bathroom noises. It was disturbing. I began to remonstrate with him over his childish behavior when he shouted a string of expletives and hung up the phone. What a rotten little kid. I wonder how old he is.

The other phone call was more promising. A young woman with a professional approach told of her interest in working in the field of modern media. She told me she was a recent graduate of Northern University with a double major in Sociology and Political Science and a minor in Journalism. Very promising indeed.

(Sorry, but I just have to say that Ob's nephew really set my teeth on edge. Somebody ought to tan his hide. Look elsewhere in this volume for more on that twit.)

Northern University. You may remember that DeWitt Clinton Overstreet III graciously provided the Commentary comment on the back cover of this volume. That is his university. I asked her: did you know him? DCO III? Yes, she told me. Well, I asked her, what did you think, did you have a class with him? She told me yes. Great, I said to her, and what was that like? She seemed reluctant to talk about this. I asked her what was up with this, you know, talking young hip to her.

"I'm afraid this will be held against me," she started. "I did not have a good experience with him. I had him for an English Composition course and I had to argue with him all the time. He has bizarre ideas." I stopped her and told her that she could say whatever she felt and it would not be held against her. I meant it. "He gave me a C for the class," she said, "and get this, I complained to the department head who changed it to an A-minus."

I told her that was too bad but that the better grade must have been satisfying. "It was," she answered, "but what was even better was when I saw him in the cafeteria, Overstreet, that is, one day and I told him to get a real job." She laughed and I joined her in the amusement. I am impressed with her spunk. And I like her outlook. Now we have a new manager for the blog. Oh, her name. I almost forgot. It's Madrid Marriott.

Before I sign off I just have to say again that C. Ob's nephew is a real piece of work. Some day somebody is going to show the rotten…well, show him which way is up.

Hiatus

(John Thom writes:)

We owe it to our legions of loyal fans and readers to tell you that this blog site will be in hiatus for a couple of weeks. The staff of creative and technical support personnel will be attending an "off-site" meeting to review where this blog has been, where it is now, and where it will be in future.

It is going to take nearly two weeks for the 3-day off-site because many of us have uncertain travel plans. We've chosen a Community Center Recreation Room in a small town in western Wisconsin near the Mighty Mississippi River. The rental fee fits in with our modest operating budget. Air fares are too high, there is no convenient train service, and bus schedules are spotty. Cars may be the only option.

We don't expect to post any additional Ob-servations during the hiatus as we won't have access to a computer in Wisconsin to the best of our knowledge. None of us has a laptop either. Those babies are real budget-busters.

We'll meet each morning from 9 a.m. to noon following some simple rules including everyone has a chance for input, all ideas are welcome and negative comments should be kept to a minimum. We will capture all the ideas on large flip-over tablets held on easels. Afternoons and evenings will be free time to allow some rest and relaxation. I think we all need it.

Constantinople Ob, our inveterate wordsmith, will not attend as his presence there could easily compromise his private life "off the grid." His absence will detract from the proceedings, to be sure, but that is a fact we'll all just have to work through.

Back From The Off-site

(John Thom writes:)
I want to tell you about the off-site meeting the blog staff held recently in Wisconsin. Let me state at the outset that we probably did not achieve as much as we hoped. There were extenuating circumstances, not least of which was the deplorable weather. (Remind me not to go to Wisconsin in the summer ever again.)

We got off to a contentious start when several staff failed to reach the town for the first day of the meeting owing to those challenging travel obstacles I had mentioned in a previous posting. Then the motel cancelled the rooms of these missing staffers and that meant a mad search for alternative accommodations. When these staffers finally found rooms, they found none had air conditioning. In Wisconsin. In the summer.

I had requested everyone to arrive at the Community Center by 8:30 a.m. so we could have coffee and donuts. There was only one donut shop in the town and apparently one of the owners' daughters was getting married about two hundred miles away. The donut shop was closed for a week.

My plan had been to nominate a different staff member to lead the brainstorming sessions each of the three days. The first-day monitor was among the missing staffers. I took over for that day and, despite a number of lulls when the ideas seemed to dry up, things turned out as well as could be expected.

The second-day session was slow to start. The night before a few of the staff had found a bar-restaurant that advertised a Happy Hour from 5 p.m. to 7 p.m. Enough said, except that the second-session morning (and the lights and the air conditioning in the meeting room) was interrupted by several lightning strikes during a rip-roaring thunderstorm. That was also the morning one of the legs of the easel holding the oversized tablet collapsed and Madrid Marriott, who was charged with taking notes, had to finish the job sitting on the floor.

You may be saying that the off-site was heading nowhere. To some extent that's true. By the end of the second morning, when the thunderstorm had spent all its power and water, all the staff had made it to the center. I was looking forward to a productive third and final morning session the next day.

That bar-restaurant? The one with the 2-hour Happy Hour? The one the staffers had discovered on the first night? They had it again this night (Happy Hour) only it was also when the officers and members of the local Rod and Gun Club got together. You know, fishermen and hunters. Fishing and hunting are big in Wisconsin.

It will have no instructive value for you if I go into the sequence of events and the details of the cultural head-knocking that ensued about halfway into Happy Hour. Suffice to say that our description of the themes and topics of C. Ob's Ob-servations met with some classic Midwestern obstinacy when we tried to inform these good folk what we were in town for. Hey, they asked.

I don't know how big a police force the town has, but if it is only three police cars and five cops, they were all on duty that evening. The guy in the gun club who was in handcuffs also had a stream of blood drying below his nose.

Unfortunately, Madrid, who has turned out to be quite a peppery sort, was also in handcuffs. "I'll follow you over to the police station," I shouted out to her as she was led away. And she said, and this was a real stunner, she said, "Don't worry about me. I've done time." That had not come up in her employment interview. Needless to say, we cancelled the third-day off-site meeting.

Our New Manager

(Madrid Marriott writes:)
Yeah, I've done time. It's no big deal. The first was a 40-day stretch that went only 20. "Good behavior," you know. It was for, get this, parking violations. Hard time for parking tickets. It was only 150 or so. Maybe 200. I think the judge had a cob up his…I think he had it in for women. Apparently also he did not cotton to my definition of "American Justice" in his courtroom…nor, I guess, to the way I described him personally. Yeah, I've done time.

The second time was better. At least it was for something from the penal code you can sink your teeth into. Disturbing the peace, drunk and disorderly, that sort of thing. It started as a bar fight. I didn't even start this one. I got 90 days and was out in 75. The prosecutor let slide the charge of assault on a police officer. He was out of uniform so who was to know?

That was the time they put me in a cell with **** ****, that actress I'm sure you have heard of. She was in for DUI and driving with a suspended license. It's like you can't be a Hollywood starlet these days and not have jail time on your resume. Anyway, she was a wreck. She cried for the first few days even though she had visitors all the time. Her mom looked like she shopped on Rodeo Drive from dawn to dark interrupted only by visits to hair salons and plastic surgeons. I think her dad was stoned every time he stopped by.

Finally, this chick got used to the routine and the other cons and the bulls and to me. We called the guards bulls. Her and me talked about things. Then we started joking about stuff. She told me how she was arrested and had to go through that field sobriety test before she was handcuffed and put into the back seat of the police car.

I told her they're called police cruisers. Then we started laughing about how in L.A. you would see a police cruiser and they all had an actor or actress in the back. I said that was how the cruisers are delivered from the car company to the police and sheriff's departments – with a rising young star hand-cuffed in the back seat as original equipment. We thought that was pretty funny.

I also got two years probation on that second one, so that's when I went back to Northern to finish college. I really had to watch my p's and q's. It wasn't so hard. There's not much to do to get into trouble in that town. And the kids at Northern...I guess you could say they didn't know how to have fun.

There. I'm glad we've cleared the air about this. It's all in the past any-way, even counting that little scrape in Wisconsin, which was not my fault in any way. Being that close to the Twin Cities, I thought those people would be Vikings fans. No. Besides, how long has somebody got to go listening to some farmer defending home-grown cheese before she asks politely that the clown put a sock in it? Politely. If I hadn't seen it "up close and personal" I would not have believed that all they do up there is talk about the Green Bay Packers and dairy products.

Hello...Brett Favre...he's gone...get used to it.

(Madrid Marriot writes:)
We now return to Con's Ob-servations from off the grid.)

Hitchhiking (I)

In my first draft of this Ob-servation I started by saying I thought hitchhik-ing had gone out of vogue. It hasn't and you can prove it by me. See, I have an admission to make. I wanted to be in attendance at this blog team's off-site meeting. As the principle author of the postings, I felt it would be good for me to listen to the ideas generated over the three days.

Unfortunately, I did not account for how long it takes to drive **** miles in this country, nor, I must also admit now, how nerve-racking thumbing rides can be. I hitchhiked from **** to western Wisconsin. In so doing I was not driving on the road all the time. Often I was merely standing on the road with my thumb out. Many people did not stop. Most actually.

I said "unfortunately" because I did not make it to western Wisconsin before the off-site meeting was prematurely cancelled. I learned later what that was all about.

The experience, however, offered other insights and rewards. I saw a slice of America I hadn't seen before and a cross-section of Americans I hadn't encountered either. You just gotta love this country. Let me share a few of the adventures I had while hitchhiking. Oh, and also, I won't be able to tell you where I was or what landmarks I was visiting or near because I live off the grid and I don't want to give away any clues as to my whereabouts.

I don't know, it was my third or fourth ride, maybe my fifth. I jumped into the pickup truck and said, "Thanks." He asked me where I was headed. I told him western Wisconsin. Where's that he wanted to know. I told him it was straight ahead for quite a ways. "Where are you going?" I asked him. "Well, now I guess to western Wisconsin," he answered. "Huh?" I thought. Then he explained that where he came from you helped people who needed help. "But," I said. "No buts about it," he said. This was a bit off-putting because after I told him I thought it was about **** miles and could take **** days, I could see he was conflicted. A few miles later we stopped at a roadside store. When my back was turned he apparently resolved his inner conflict. I did not see him again.

In **** just outside ****, a nice couple picked me up and because it was close to "suppertime" and darkness would be falling soon they invited me to spend the night with them. I wish now I hadn't accepted.

My sense of comfort gave way to misgivings even before we ate when they asked me to give thanks for the meal. So I said "thanks." Not what they meant. "A prayer," someone said, actually it was sneered. I don't know any prayer like that by heart and as we were joined in a hand-holding circle around the supper table with their three grown sons and a "kissin cousin," all four of whom had not spoken a word since I entered the house, I couldn't even think of saying, "Thank you, God." Seeing I was not on speaking terms with the Lord at that minute, the missus kindly broke in.

"Marvin," she announced, would say grace. No one spoke. "Marvin," she announced again, would say the prayer. Still no one spoke. "Oh," she said, "did I say Marvin? He can't say the prayer, he's dead these 15 years." One of the sons finally spoke. "He woulda been alive these 15 years now if you hadn't had them pull the cord on that machine that done his breathing for him."

The two on either side of me squeezed my hands. We were, after all, still in a hand-holding circle. "He wouldna needed that there machine if you hadna hit him with the tractor," the missus countered. "I wouldna hit him with the tractor if he hadna been hidin in the haystack with that Annabelle whore." "She weren't no whore, she done that for free." "She always made me give her fifty cent." "She still does, you ass. Why'd you marry her anyway?" The mister broke in. "Somebody thank God for the vittles soon or we'll all starve." The circle broken, finally, my hands were aching and were full of sweat. I ate, but I didn't enjoy it.

I'll stop here for now, but I will continue with some of my hitchhiking adventures in Ob-servations real soon.

Hitchhiking (II)

Here is more from my hitchhiking adventure to western Wisconsin. Another day I got a ride in a pickup truck from the **** end of the **** Bridge across the **** River where **** and **** have their state boundaries. The fellow was about 50 years old wearing only boots and cutoff Levis. He wasn't wearing a shirt. He seemed to be a fan of tattoos.

"Hotteren hell, ain't it?" he asked in a way that didn't seem to want an answer. "How far ya goin?" he called out to me from two feet away. "Western Wisc…" "Cause I'm only goin as far as ****." "Thanks," I said. "I'm not goin no furtheran that," he continued. "Only to ****." "Thanks," I said.

After he picked me up he sped back into the light traffic and pulled up behind another car so close I thought we were going to hit it. "Does this fucker think he's in a funeral convoy or what?" he suddenly shouted. Honk, honk, honk, he slammed into his horn. The car in front sped up a little. Honk, honk, honk, my driver repeated.

That's when the "excitement" started. The driver of the car in front of us shot his arm and hand out his window and made a familiar gesture with one of his fingers. My driver responded in kind. The other driver tapped on his brakes forcing my driver to brake quickly before speeding again to catch up to the other driver who had pulled over into another lane.

"Open that up and give it to me," my driver yelled, pointing at the glove compartment in front of me. "Wha?" "There, right there, open it up." I did. There was a bottle of bourbon or whiskey or something. "This is no time to drink," I admonished him. "I don't want no fuckin drink, you shithead, gimme that," he shouted. Behind the bottle was a gun.

"You want that? What for?" "To pick my teeth with, whaddya think? Just give it to me." "No." Instead of arguing, he leaned over and grabbed the gun from the glove compartment in such a way that it occurred to me he'd done this more than once before.

"Roll down your window," he yelled at me. "Wha?" "Roll down your goddam window." "No," I said. "I don't wanna shoot through the glass. I've had to replace it three or four times already. Roll it down." He was still shouting. "Let me out first." "Naw, then I won't never catch back up. Just roll down your fuckin window." I didn't care for the rough type of language he was using. It was as shocking as some of his tattoos, one of which read, "I'm over 18, honey, and so are you."

The gun was waving madly through the air as my driver held the steering wheel with one hand. The other car was along side of us. I was ready for a classic anxiety attack.

"Let me reason with that fellow," I said. "I'll show you reason," my driver said. "Wait a moment," I said as I rolled down the window. "We're sorry," I shouted over to the driver of the other car, "we'll just drop back and forget the whole thing." I guess he couldn't hear me because his response was unexpected. His left arm came out of his car window with a gun of his own.

I don't know how many shots were fired, but the fact that not one of us was hit is nothing less than Dame Fortune at work. The other car left the highway at a turn up ahead. My driver put his gun back into the glove compartment. "Hey," he said, "there's a great saloon up the road. You can buy me a beer. You know what they say, 'There ain't no free rides, even for hitchhikers'."

One beer turned into six for him. I drank about half of one. Later, after I lost a debate with myself about going on with him in his pickup, he dropped me off at a promising interchange. As he drove off I noticed he had a bumper sticker on his trunk (because he had no bumper). It read, "Impeach 'em all."

Once again I'll stop here, but I promise to return to my hitchhiking adventures in future Ob-servations because I have a suspicion you'll find, like me, that America offers a kaleidoscope of shapes and colors.

Hitchhiking (III)

You will remember that I was telling you about my hitchhiking adventures when I went to western Wisconsin to attend this blog team's off-site meeting. Which I missed. The meeting, not western Wisconsin. Before I got there, to western Wisconsin, I got a ride with an elderly gentleman who, if he wasn't eighty-five years old, was ninety or more. I was in a truck stop in **** on Hwy ****.

The day before I was a hundred miles away in **** when the sky turned gray then clouded over to near black before it let loose with a thunderstorm which, to me, was biblical in its rage. Water coursed down the streets, up over curbs, and raced into the **** River raising its banks lightning quick. And speak of lightning! Streaks and bolts every few seconds followed by thunder that shook the very earth beneath me. I was terrified, and I don't scare easily.

At the truck stop the elderly gentleman said he was going my direction and I could join him. I learned he had been in the same thunderstorm, and when I told him how fearsome I thought it was he said, "Aw, that was just a summer drizzle. You would know different if you had been around these parts in '58, or was it '59. That was the big one. It floated Bernice and her brood right up onto the roof. They had to get row boats out there to get them down."

It took Eugene (that was my driver's name and he told me that about a dozen times, asking me mine each time) at least a minute and a half to tell me what I just reported to you because he talked very slowly and his bridge fell loose at least three times.

"Is Bernice your wife?" I asked Eugene. "Bernice?" he answered. I didn't know what to say. I started to repeat my question when he began. "Bernice? Bernice was mother's sister. She was wedded to Roger who died in 1951. It was cancer. Cancer took his brother, too. That was Vernon. That was in 1953. Bernice re-married to one of the Millers from ****. That was Carlton because his wife died in 1949 from the auto accident just outside **** on the **** hill that takes you past the Stockton farm.

"They sold that farm and moved to Florida. To Sarasota, I think, where Charlie Stockton's sons were in the insurance business. They both graduated from the University of ****. They went through pharmacy school but they found they could make more money in the insurance business. The Shuttlehorns do the insurance business where I live and…"

About two hours later he dropped me in the center of **** where I was glad to be rid of such a nice man, but one who told me more about people I'd never met than I know about the people in my own family. I heard him going on with the story as he drove away.

I think I've got one more Ob-servation on my hitchhiking trip, so I'll stop here and get that other one ready for you.

Hitchhiking (IV)

My last ride into the town in Wisconsin where I thought I would be joining this blog team's off-site meeting was in a flatbed truck, no, not that, a stakebed truck. Yes, stakebed, loaded up with fruits and vegetables. Two very nice young ladies were headed to a weekly Farmer's Market in the town square.

I say they were very nice, and they were at the start. I should also tell you that they were both very handsome in a womanly sort of way. After one thing led to another, one of them said to the other, "You were out with him again last night, weren't you?" "What if I was?" said the other. "I told you to leave hands off him." "And I told you I can put my hands anywhere I feel."

The stakebed truck has a large driver's compartment and for some reason the two women had decided I should sit in the middle of the seat between them for the ride into town.

"Not on him, you can't." "Watch me." "He ain't yours to touch." "He don't seem to mind." "He's too dumb to mind." "He is when he's with you." There was no comradeship in the conversation. I said, "Excuse me…" but that's all. "Hush," one of them said. "Yeah, hush," said the other. They meant it. I hushed.

"I'm going to talk to him. Give me your cell." "Use your own damn cell." "I don't got it with me. Give me your damn cell." She, for reasons I cannot explain, gave her her damn cell.

It was the driver who was dialing the cell phone. We were going about 50 mph and the driver was ignoring the roadway. As we drifted across the centerline, the other lady leaned past me, grabbed the steering wheel and propelled us back into our own lane. The driver kept dialing.

"Leave the wheel to me," the driver snapped at the other. "I don't wanna die on Hwy ****, you bitch, so I'll grab it if I wanna." "Me the bitch? You're the one who…hello, Sebastian, is that you?" (Pause.) "Yeah, good, I'm fine." (Pause.) "To the Farmer's Market like every week." (Pause.) "Well, maybe three, four hundred bucks if it don't rain." (Pause.) "Never mind about my… about that. You were out again last night, right?" (Pause.) "What kind of answer is that?" (Pause.) "Sebastian, just tell me…" (Pause.) "Yeah, she's with me." (Pause.) "Hold on."

"He wants to talk to you." The other one took the phone. "Hi, Sebastian." (Pause.) "To the Farmer's Market like every week." (Pause.) "I don't know." (Pause.) "I said I don't know, maybe a couple of hundred bucks." (Pause.) "Well, maybe." (Pause.) "Hold on. What's that?" (Pause.) "Jeezus, Sebastian, never mind about my…about that. You're so dirty" – she giggled – "hold on." She handed the cell back to the driver.

"Sebastian." (Pause.) "You are the biggest fuckin liar I've ever seen." (Pause.) "Shit, that's another lie." (Pause.) "Maybe I won't be around the next time you call." (Pause.) "Yes." (Pause.) "Hey, what's your name?" Nothing happened for a moment. "I said what's your name." Nothing happened again. "I said," and here's when her elbow went cutting into my ribs, "what's your name?" "Who, me?" I said. "Well, who else?" "Constantinople." "What?" "Constantinople." Both pretty ladies began laughing. Then the driver said, "Here take this," handing me the cell. "I don't want to…" "Take it. Talk to Sebastian."

"Hello," I said. "Who's this?" Sebastian demanded. "I'm just along for the ride," I said truthfully. "Well, hot damn, just along for the ride, huh? Well, let me tell you something. I'm about half a mile behind you and when I find you I'm going to cut off your…" I didn't hear very much of the rest of that because I stared at the phone and then I dropped it onto the floor.

"Let me out," I cried out to the two women.

"Did he try to scare you? He's always doing that. What did he say?"

I repeated as best I could what Sebastian had said. They laughed. "That's a good one, but his favorite is to tell guys that he'll unscrew your head and piss down your neck. He's a little jealous of us, so don't worry. He's on probation and if he has any more…" and here the other woman broke in to finish the thought. "…fracases he'll have to go before that judge again. And the judge is running out of patience with Sebastian. The judge is his brother-in-law."

The names of the two ladies were Sharon and Sheree. They looked like sisters. Come to reflect on it, they looked like twins, but one had blonde hair and the other had red hair. Can that be? Can twins have different hair colors? That's interesting.

I never did meet Sebastian. That did not disappoint me.

Space

Now they're saying something that even I find hard to believe, and I like to think of myself as open-minded. Where do they come up with this stuff? This new something, get this, they're saying there's "dark matter" all over the place. Yeah. Only they can't really show us any. Seems it started a long time ago, at the beginning they say, you know, billions of years ago when there was the Big Bang. Then a few minutes later (someone must have been wearing a watch) there was all this "dark matter" tossed about, in fact way more than of anything else.

Who do they think we are, just some rookies who will hear this kind of talk and jump on their bandwagon no questions asked? I'm not from Missouri, but I'll be one for a day – a Missourian – and proclaim proudly, "I want to see it." Wait one, is that what Missourians say? No, it's "Show Me." There. Same idea.

They sit in their little ivory towers (scientists, not Missourians) and punch in numbers on their computers and draw pictures of galaxies that indicate all sorts of business doings. Have they ever gone to one to test their artistic theories? I think not.

Instead they do go to Europe and hold "scientific conferences" and read their papers and show off their pictures and have a swell time. They love to toss out names, too. Albert Einstein, Isaac Newton, Bill Nye. All that does is cloud the issue, if you want my opinion.

Not only are they saying these things, but also they're getting huge amounts of money from who knows where to build big apparatuses to test their assertions. If I weren't living off the grid and disinclined to interact with my government, I would write a sharply worded letter to my congressman demanding he check this out. You know, are there tax dollars involved here? Maybe my congressman isn't a man. Maybe he's a congresswoman. I don't know.

What I am going to say next should not come as a surprise to anyone reading this Ob-servation, and I just hope you'll see the irony in it, even the humor, that I see. Here it is: there is another band of scientists who don't agree with the crowd promoting these "dark matter" ideas. (Where do you suppose they're getting *their* funding to promulgate *their* notions about this? I'm one who wants to know.)

Does it always have to come down to money? You'd think so, wouldn't you, if you watched these birds go about their shenanigans. But no, there's also the whole "ego" thing. Einstein, Newton? You throw those names into your presentation and people start to pay attention. Painting yourself with the same brush as the masters tends to inflate your own stature in the scientific community.

I could do that, too. Drop great names from the literary community like Shakespeare, Chaucer, Twain, Aesop (uh-huh, right). But I won't because a serious examination of a subject like this deserves a serious editorial evenness.

I happened recently to be eating a late lunch at Tito's Tacos and a college-age chap sat down and we talked very informally for a few minutes before I mentioned off-handedly how I'd read something about "dark matter."

"Oh," he said, "yeah, right, it's everywhere. I'm an astrophysics major at **** (a university). I'm learning, like, all about it." I had no response. The kid was obviously not from Missouri. I couldn't have responded conveniently anyhow because he kept talking. I listened. He was enjoying himself, talking about his passion.

Toward the end I was able to get a word in edgewise. "Isn't something this complicated impossible to prove?" "No," he said, "we will some day, if we get enough funding. Besides, it really isn't complicated at all. Let me draw a parallel," he went on. "It's like when you take up golf and you discover just how simple the golf swing is. Am I right or what?"

His interesting choice of comparisons made the whole thing come clear to me. So now I know this whole thing about "dark matter" is plain bunk. You see, I've tried golf. There's no such thing as a "simple swing." That's also bunk.

A Correction

It was a senior moment of the first order. Here I was writing about one thing and I mentioned where I was eating when an event happened. Yes, I was having a Mexican meal. I happen to favor *el Mexicana comida*, as I like to call it. (I speak a little Mexican.) And as I have had, in my "on the grid" past, a favorite Mexican restaurant, I wrote down that name as the one I was in. A senior moment to be sure.

And I'm not even a senior.

You see, and bear with me on this, please, I am living off the grid as you know, and that means I cannot leave any clues as to my whereabouts. If I did, well, I don't even want to speculate on all the possible traumatic outcomes.

So when I wrote in my "Space" Ob-servation recently that I was having a late lunch at Tito's Tacos, that was just a slip of the pen. Sure, I have a long relationship with Tito's, an enormously popular Mexican restaurant there in

Culver City, California, a suburb of Los Angeles near where I lived before going off the grid. It was natural for me to think those happy thoughts as I ate my taco, cheese enchilada, beans and chips. Only natural. Oh, and a root beer. Tito's isn't licensed.

I blame myself for this. I wrote what I wrote and I didn't catch the mistake when I went back over the essay during my usual proofreading moments. Now it's in the past and let's just put an end to it. No more talk about where I may live or may not live or where I eat. It's a closed book. Come to think about it, I guess this is not really "A Correction," just an explanation. What the hey, right?

A Statue

In a moment I will tell you which little town I'm talking about, and when I do, this will all become much clearer than it may appear at first glance.

Where most of you come from you probably already have a statue in the Town Square of a locally famous military man riding upon a horse in one of several poses. This town doesn't have such a statue. That's about to change if you believe the town council and some local merchants who feel, quite solemnly, disadvantaged.

All this in spite of the upsetting revelations by the librarian and amateur – and unofficial – town historian. She claims the town has no military heroes who rode horses. The town council, in an uncontrolled episode of pique, brought up the old rumor of her affinity for distilled spirits. That was uncalled for at the time even though someone – no one would admit to it – said it was "politics as usual."

Everyone who has followed this proposal to have a statue erected could easily relate the yin and yang it has fostered. It is not the fault of the news people alone, but it hasn't helped that the Weekly Clarion has gone through three ownership changes in the past 18 months. Why? Because each owner has taken a different editorial view of "Statuegate." This has left readers unsure of their own opinions. Newspapers, after all, can have that type of influence.

What is agreed is where a statue is best positioned for the town. About a block past the third traffic light on the main street into town from the north-south 4-lane highway there is an old-fashioned traffic circle. Five different streets radiate from the circle to other parts of town. Many businesses have stores nearby.

The grassy knoll in the circle is a near unanimous choice for the statue. If there is to be a statue.

———◆———

I have an admission to make. This is where my Ob-servation stood a few months ago before I moved off the grid. Nothing much was happening with the statue issue and, honestly, I was becoming preoccupied with my own future.

Now it can be told. After I made my decision about my future, the town got its ducks in a row and chose a local hero for the statue.

But can you believe it? Now there is a whole new controversy. The statue is designed, built and erected. It is a horse and the chosen hero is depicted riding upon it. Such was the luck, however, that this hero was a 12-year-old state spelling bee champion who made it to the final eight in the national spell-offs. He was a precocious young fellow. He was also a pixie of a young man who barely filled a saddle. The horse on the other hand was of stouter stock, or at least that is how the ironmonger who built it saw it.

Then there is the concrete base upon which the horse stands. The base is easily six feet off the ground. Then you've got a horse easily 16 hands high. You are craning your neck to get a good view of the statue. That's where the controversy comes in. The view. The horse is facing west into the sunset. Traffic on that road, meanwhile, heads west toward that circle. The commanding view is of the horse's posterior and a mighty one it is.

Ms. Bunting-Lewis, she's our librarian/historian, often recommends to visitors to drive out there to see the statue and admire what she calls, "Welcome to Horse Hole." The name of the town is, more accurately, Horseman's Hollow Township.

Exclusive Interview

(Madrid Marriott writes:)

The following Q and A is an exclusive interview with Constantinople Ob who has been living "off the grid" for several months. This lifestyle choice, this phenomenon, caught the public's attention when New York Times best-selling author John Twelve Hawks revealed that he himself lives off the grid. His whereabouts and his true identity are known, it appears, only to himself and perhaps a handful of others. So too for C. Ob, author of the Ob-servations which make up the content of this blog. John Thom (JT) and I (MM) posed the questions via telephone to C. Ob (CO) knowing that he would refuse to answer in any way those that might give his location away. He also took measures to cloak his identity during the interview and this led to some technical problems with the audio taping which will be apparent in parts of the transcript. The length of the interview and space considerations on the blog determined that we present it in more than one posting.

JT: Hello, Con, are you there?
CO: Yesh.
JT: Good. First, it's good to be in touch with you. Your many readers will certainly want me to ask how you are doing.
CO: Fine, I'm doing ine.
JT: Good. Fine. Where are you now?
CO: I won't ans that because I don't (-) to open (-) avenue to where I half gone to.
JT: Oh, of course, how stupid of me to ask. I can be so dim.
CO: Perhaps. Lesh move on.
MM: Your Ob-servations continue to arrive on schedule. Do you find inspiration for them living off the grid?
CO: Yesh and no. I still she life's panorama in (-) same way (-) before, though I must (-) not to write something that would eaten my anonymity. I still fry to be an honest writer, but I am also still uning (-) my new lifestyle to influence my Ob-servation popics and content. You know I'm a politic

in the convent since even while a communist critic of the authoritary in landscape.

MM: Little tough to make out what you are saying there. The connection doesn't seem to be too good. What obstacles do you face living off the grid?

CO: There are some, a few, but I antidepressant them for the most port. I don't have credit card, no checking amount, no driver's license, no car, no cellophane, no passport, well, I do (-), but I will not be using it. I don't have a computer, no (-) to the Innernet. When I do want to go on line I use a computer at my loyal library ranch. I use my library car for that but they don't keel a record of my computer use. Oh, and I've growed a beard.

MM: Again, a little tough to make out all your words. How do you communicate? Certainly there are those you have to have dealings with.

CO: As muck as possibly I do it fash to fash. I stare a post office ox with a friend. I use pubic paper telephones when calling is necessary. I carry loafs of quarters. I sound like a cement mixer when I walk.

JT: Do you go by your own name?

CO: No, that would be feet the holy idea of anonymity and slaying off the grid, wouldn't I?

JT: Yes, I see. Another stupid question. Gad, what's wrong with me today? Sorry.

MM: As I understand it, you and John Twelve Hawks are the only authors who have acknowledged living this new lifestyle.

CO: And? That's not a question.

MM: Oh, right. Well, are you? The only two?

CO: I don't (-)

MM: I'm sorry. You cut out there. What did you say?

CO: I don't know.

MM: You don't know what you said or you don't know about other authors?

CO: Yeah, the second one.

MM: Do you meet anyone else who is living off the grid?

CO: I don't know. We don't wear badges. We don't hope monthly meetings.

MM: Of course. Here, John has another question.

JT: Have you met anyone else who is living off the grid?

CO: Huh?

MM: I just asked him that.

CO: Aren't you lispering? You use to be more attendance.

JT: Oh, for heaven's sake. I've got to pull myself together.

(This seemed like a good place to stop the first installment of the interview. It will resume in this space shortly.)

Exclusive Interview (II)

(Continuing the interview with Constantinople Ob who is living off the grid, we pick up the Q and A where we left off last time.)

MM: When you write your Ob-servations, who do you see as your principal reader or audience?

CO: High cool graduates entering college.

MM: Hmmm. That seems unusual. Why them?

CO: Because they will be (-) book buying frenzy.

MM: That's a bit commercial, isn't it?

CO: Yesh. Tank you.

MM: Do you still see the world as stacked up against you?

CO: Well, yes, if you bean is everything the shame as before I mooed off the grid. But (-) snot the world stacked up again me, as you like it. It's the vast Othellian frame...

MM: That did not sound clear to me. Can you repeat that?

CO: The vast authoritarian frameword again us. Olive us. Here's a sample one to contemple. When you boo a tango gasoline with your credit card at a bill nation, why are you bequested to pumpkin your Zip Code? Why does the biggedst oil company in the world, for example, need to know that? Have you taught about that?

MM: I think it's because...

CO: It's because they can tackle your movement, your driving habit, your purchasing figurtaries. What's next, crayola implants in your head with Jeeps and bar codes? And another thing…

MM: I'm sorry, you're breaking up there. Is there something wrong with the phone at your end?

CO: No. I'm holding a hangershift over my mouth.

MM: You're doing what?

CO: Hold a hankie over my mouth.

MM: Whatever for?

CO: I live off the grid, madame, and I do not want to do anything that will helt reseal anything about me or where I am.

JT: You know, Con, that I already know who you are, and we will be uploading this on the blog. No one will hear your voice or know where you are.

CO: I'm the one who lives off the grid, so I'm the one who bake the tools.

JT: Well, have it your way. The transcript is going to look a little haywire, if you ask me.

CO: Who asked you?

MM: Pardon the interruption, but you sound a bit out of sorts. Is it anything we have said?

CO: What it is is this living style is not so easy. I'm still king on witing my Ob-servations, but to do so I half Dubai pens and tablets because I just can't truss computers. Then it's alldays clocking over my shoulder, so to speak. I don't know whobybe back there. Remember the old yoke that even paranoiacs have enemies.

MM: Are you saying your commitment is wavering?

CO: (Unintelligible.)

MM: Sorry, did not get that.

CO: (Sniff…cough) (Unintelligible.)…and I don't know if or when.

(This seemed like a good place to stop the second installment of the interview. It will resume in this space shortly.)

Exclusive Interview (III)

(Continuing the interview with Constantinople Ob, who is living off the grid, we pick up the Q and A where we left off last time.)

MM: I missed almost all of that.

JT: What did he say?

MM: I don't know.

JT: Con, can you put that hankie down? We're having trouble getting your answers.

CO: (Sniff.) I put it down a few moments ago.

MM: (Laughing.) I think he's crying.

JT: Are you crying?

CO: Let's move on.

MM: Okay, of course. Good. Okay, umm, what do you miss most now that you are off the grid?

CO: Good question. There's real irony in this. You know what it is? It's the easy way to accomplish things even though I am full suspicious of the motives of those providers. Like a driver's license, credit cards, leaving my name at a restaurant with a reservation, shopping for an easy chair, e-mail, escort services, a banking relationship, airline travel. Did you know I wanted some time to just kick back and I thought of taking a cruise? Then I looked at the application. I would have had to reveal more to a sailing company than to the IRS. It's dismaying.

MM: Escort services?

CO: Let's move on.

JT: A cruise? Where?

CO: Hell, I don't know. What difference does it make? The Panama Canal?

JT: That'd be nice.

CO: For you maybe, but not for me and John Twelve Hawks.

JT: Really? Do you know him?

MM: We've been down that road, Mr. T.

JT: Yes, indeed. Sorry.

MM: Do I detect any misgivings on your part?

JT: No, I...

MM: Not you, John.

JT: Oh.

CO: Not at present.

MM: At this end we hope that we will continue to receive your Ob-servations. We will, won't we?

CO: That's my plan.

MM: Do you have a social life?

CO: A social life? What do you mean?

MM: I assume you are not in hiding in some unconventional sense. You interact with others, I hope. Do you meet women?

CO: Oh, I see. Sure. In fact there's a wonderful little bar-café not far from where I'm living which has a friendly stream of regulars and you're made to feel at home whenever you're there. I like it. There's a half dozen television sets showing a variety of sporting and news events. A jukebox with a nice selection of newer and older popular music. Three pool tables, too, and I'm getting a little better on those. Oh, and a popcorn machine. Hot popcorn for free.

MM: That doesn't sound only like fun, but also it sounds very familiar. Is it...

CO: Hold on!

MM: Ooops. Sorry. I didn't mean to turn detective on you.

JT: That's Hinano's down in Venice Beach, isn't it?

CO: Oh, great galloping Zeus! Are you mad? Are you for real?

JT: What?

MM: I think he means his anonymity should come first.

JT: Oh. Did I...What have I done?

MM: Not to worry, we can excise those few questions and comments. No one will know. You can remain protected.

JT: Yeah, protected. I'm real sorry.

CO: Oh, screw it. I'm coming back. Onto the grid. I'll fight the bastards the old-fashioned way, out in the open. With ink.

JT: What great news. We'll be so glad to see you again. What made you change your mind?

MM: Oh, John, you're just precious.

CO: Thanks, Madrid. I'm looking forward to meeting you.

MM: Likewise, Con, I'm sure.

Lapse

(John Thom writes:)

Here's the explanation for the lapse in postings at this blog. There's been a little disconnect for a while with C. Ob, M. Marriott and me. Except, that is, for a short post C. Ob provided just after revealing he was going to return from off the grid. You'll recall that decision from his announcement at the end of the exclusive interview we conducted with him.

Oh, fudge, I'll just say it. We still don't know where he is. I'm afraid Madrid has gone missing as well. I have no clues as to what's going on with either of them. Happily, I have no evidence that there has been any wrongdoing or an accident. I simply don't know.

I said Constantinople had supplied a short posting. In it he declared he was back, that it was his choice, but that his new adopted lifestyle had, well, heck, let me just reprint it for you here:

> "It's true. I am back. I no longer live off the grid. It's my choice, just as it was my choice earlier this year to go underground. Living off the grid was my statement about the many intrusive forces enveloping us, threatening our privacy and independence. Returning is a more practical choice.
>
> "Frankly, it wasn't easy off the grid. That hitchhiking trip to Wisconsin was a real eye opener. I learned that my calling to blog the Ob-servations of our day was being blunted by that lifestyle. 'Lifestyle,' and isn't that a joke?
>
> "I am content to be back to an open schedule and a conventional routine, which will allow me to concentrate on meaty Ob-servation topics. I plan to get back into them immediately.

"Oh, yes, John Thom and I have determined also that Madrid Marriott should continue as the everyday blog manager. She has good editorial skills and knows her way around computers and cyberspace.

"To conclude, as the Germans say, C'est la guerre. That's for John Twelve Hawks, whoever and wherever you are."

(John Thom writes further:)

I learned that I had concurred in the decision to retain Madrid Marriott as blog manager the same way as you, by reading it in one of those last paragraphs from Ob. I guess I'm okay with it. Don't even ask me to explain his last comment about what Germans say. And that Hawks character.

I like a mystery as much as the next guy, or gal, except when I'm a part of it. I don't like this. What's to become of the blog if something has happened to Con? Oh yeah, and to Madrid? My travel obligations prevent me from taking an active role in the planning or the carrying-out of the Ob-servations. As fans, you will appreciate the unique contributions from Con. He is central to the whole affair. I am going to sign off now. I am going to try to clear my head. I may even call the police.

Missing Persons

(John Thom still writing:)

I called the police. Told them (him actually) that my friend was missing. Got transferred to Missing Persons. Told this one my friend was missing. Friend? What kind of friend? Well, just the usual kind, I suppose. Name. I gave it. No, not yours, the missing guy's. I gave it. What kind of name is that anyway? I really couldn't answer. Thought he was your friend. He is. How long's he been missing? About a week. That's the last time you saw him? No. When then? About four or five months ago. Is this a prank call? No. You haven't seen him in half a year but he's been missing only a week? Yes. Do you want to explain that?

I explained. Constantinople is missing, etc.

"Off the grid, huh? Let me tell you something, mister. Filing a false police report is a serious matter, and if I were you I'd hang up the phone right now and thank my lucky stars I reached a policeman on desk duty today who has a sense of humor."

"But it's all true. What I explained to you. What's more, Madrid is missing, too," I said to the officer.

There was a silence for moment. Then, "Sir, over here at the police department we have technology to help us serve you better. One of those is a system to track just who it is who calls us. That helps us serve you better. Today, ironically, it is going to help serve *me* better. I now have your phone number, your address and your name."

"But…"

"So don't call again saying you have lost an old city and a current city. That may sound like a funny joke where you are from, but not here. Lucky stars, remember? Start counting."

I didn't count. I did hang up. A day or so later in walks Con. "Where have you been?" "Off the grid, you know that." "No, I mean since you said you were coming back; I called the police." "I had a few things to do; you called the police?" "I thought you were missing." "Why?" "You weren't here." "I told you, I had a few things to do."

Well, maybe I jumped the gun there a little. It was different with Madrid. She showed up a day later. "Where have you been?" "I was busy." "Busy?" "Yes." "I was worried." "You needn't be, it was just one of those things I have to do from time to time." At which she giggled.

I pressed her for an explanation. You'd think that owning a blog site would be a lot easier than this was turning out to be. She explained. I'll paraphrase. She went "clubbing" one evening about a week before. Had a couple of drinks. Danced. Saw a gaggle of young women, you know, professional party-goers, some of whom have made headlines in recent years. There was some taunting. One bodyguard got a little pushy. He went down (Madrid said with some glee.) There was some additional "conversation and only a small amount of blood" and then everybody got friendly.

The party moved to a house in the hills, Madrid being invited. She promised she was watching her p's and q's because she is still on probation. The party got loud and more rambunctious. At about the third day of this and the appearance of local police several times, Madrid decided she didn't want to risk being arrested along with her new friends. In fact, she said, by this time there were only one or two of the original band of party-goers. "I have a lot more staying power than most," she boasted.

That bodyguard she popped came back and together they drove to Vegas where she won about eleven hundred dollars at a craps table. Con heard the whole story, too. He said, "She's a hoot and a half, isn't she?" I don't need hoots. Or half hoots. I need Constantinople Ob to write his Ob-servations and Madrid Marriott to post them efficiently. That's when I can count my lucky stars.

(John Thom writes:)
This ends the section of Ob-servations and reports having to do with C. Ob's period of life off the grid. We return to his normal Ob-servations. I think you will agree with this statement, however: there is nothing normal about them at all.

The Ob-servations
Themselves, More Of

A First Time For Everything

When the guy on your bowling team shouts out, "There's a first time for everything," after someone scores a strike, he's just being sarcastic. It's just the way he is. I don't know why we asked him to be on our team. He's a below average bowler anyway. Maybe he's someone's brother-in-law. But he raises a point. The "first time" for something. Like the first person to order escargot. There's a wonder. Why wasn't he also the last person for that one?

No, what I am thinking about is the ophthalmologist who tells a patient it is time for the first cataract surgery. Of course the patient's initial question is not how soon can we schedule *that*, rather it is what is a cataract. After the eye doc defines the term and the problem, the patient's interest balloons.

"That's part of my eye, what do you plan to do to it?" After the eye doc answers that one, the patient's interest runs to how soon can I get out of his office. Being a kindly soul with a charming bedside manner and a gift for choosing just the right words, the doctor persuades the patient to trust in his diagnosis. He says, "What, you wanna go blind, you damn fool?"

It is decided. The operation will be the middle of next month. That gives the patient a few weeks to have nightmares centering on a pointy stick hurtling toward his eye. Every night. Also a prescription is written for eye drops to be used up to the day of surgery. Eye drops. Not stiff drinks. How does the doctor know that eye drops are going to be of any use when he has no previous experience to fall back on? This is the first cataract operation, right? Stiff drinks, on the other hand, have volumes of history written to show their effectiveness.

The patient knows this other fellow who shows his own interest in the novel medical procedure. "This is the first time ever, is it?" the fellow says. "I know a little something about that feeling. So what's the doctor going to do?"

The description of the procedure by the patient is not word for word from what the doctor told him. It's a transliteration, one seasoned by the trepidations most patients face when "going under the knife." He answered, "The doctor is going to slice the front of my eye and rip out the lens. Then he's going to plug in a new one and glue it in place and then solder it closed all around. I guess he does some other things as well, but I forget what they are because I started to lose consciousness around 'rip out the lens'."

The other fellow considered this and asked, "And he's never done this before? No one has? It's mighty brave of him to try this."

"Him brave," the patient expresses, "what about me? It's my eye."

The other fellow says, "Yes, but when it's over, it's over."

"I have the other eye done in a month."

The other fellow reeled. "You are going to do it again? Wow. I thought up until now that we were a lot alike."

"What do you mean?"

"Well, I can lay claim to a 'first time for everything' occurrence, too."

"Yeah, what?"

"I'm the first person to order escargot."

"You!"

"Uh-huh. Only I wasn't dumb enough to order it a second time."

Ducks And Drakes

I'm not one to boast, but I think you'll forgive a little bragging when I say that *Word for Word* is awfully useful, or will be once a sensible publisher comes to its senses and pays for the rights. Sorry that we co-editors are so repetitive about this, but, gracious, when will it happen?

I say brag because I had a role in its development. But that's not what I want to talk about. The point is you could look it up right there under "D" in *Word for Word* (you know, if the thing had been published) and see for yourself. It says it is "a pastime of almost universal appeal and application with youths and most adults, of whom almost none can actually call it by its proper name." Pretty useful definition, what?

I don't recall at this minute which of the co-editors had the most input into this entry. I'll wager it was one who had a passion for the out-of-doors. Oh, I remember now. It was that kid. Lester? No, that's not his name. Les…Lex, yes, Lex E. Kahn. A bit of a snotnose at times, if you get my drift. And that mother of his, what a budinski, always around looking after him. Between them I think they don't have the brains of a woodpile.

Anyway he told the story how he learned about this pastime and what it is called. He was at a summer camp in the local mountains and (oh, sorry, I'm going to tell this story in my own words and with my descriptions. You see, this kid told what I would call a lousy story. Always I, I, I. Anyway it will still be accurate as to what he went through.) Let's see…at a camp…in the mountains…yes, okay, and there was a lake.

So he goes off on his own one day to the lake. I don't think he was supposed to leave the camp site unchaperoned. Knowing him as I do now, that would be him all over. Moreover, I would not be the least surprised to learn that none of the other campers had any interest in playing with him.

So he's at the lake with no one to play with and no toys or anything. He picks up a rock and throws it into the lake. Big splash. He does it again. Big splash again. Then he tries to throw a rock that will bounce on the water. Rocks will do that (if you aren't a retard like Lex.) He throws it and it doesn't skip, it just sinks. Then he notices there's an older fellow standing at the tree line back from the water. He (Les…er, Lex) keeps trying to bounce rocks on the lake but all they'll do is sink. Then the man in the trees says, "Having trouble?"

Lex says, "Bugger off."

"No need for billingsgate, lad."

"Lex, not lad, and bugger off anyway."

"I noticed you were trying to skip the rocks you were throwing. Am I right?"

"Maybe you're right, maybe you're not. What's it to you?"

"I can teach you how to do it."

"I can learn on my own."

"You haven't had any luck yet."

"What makes you so good at it?"

"I learned from someone who took the trouble to teach me."

"Aren't you a lucky ass." (I told you he was a snotnose.)

"Okay, sorry I interrupted your game," the man said.

"It's not a game."

"Yes, it is."

"Oh, yeah, what's it called?"

"I'd be remiss if I told you what it is called if you didn't even know how to do it." The snotnose apparently paused here and considered his circumstances.

"Okay," he finally said.

"Okay what?" the man at the tree line said.

"Okay, teach me."

"Teach me what?"

"How to play this dumb game. What'd you think?"

"No, I mean what's the magic word?" Recognizing this question as the one whose answer is "please," the snotnose kid used a dirty term here which I will not include.

"That kind of talk is not necessary," the man in the tree line responded.

"Are you going to teach me or not?"

"Sure, okay."

The man at the tree line walked down to Lex, looking at the rocks on the ground. He found one he liked and showed it to Lex. "Do you see how this has two flat sides? When you toss it onto the lake, throw it like this (he demonstrated a sidearm approach) so the flat side hits the water first. Then it'll skip."

Lex proceeded to throw a flat-sided rock onto the lake and it skipped several times just as it had for the man who had been at the tree line but was now standing next to Lex.

"Good one. Now I can tell you what this game is called."

"Can you?"

"Yes, it's called Ducks and Drakes."

"Do you know what I am going to call you when I get back to my camp?" Lex asked the man standing next to him.

"No, what?"

"Child molester."

The man standing next to Lex reportedly ran back very fast into the trees and disappeared.

(Rebuttal by Anna Kahn, Lex's mother:)
Somebody told me I should read this particular "Ob-servation," that it would do me some good. If that doesn't just poach my eggs. Making up this awful stuff about my Lex. I knew there was something funny about this Ob character. Somebody ought to give him a good kick on his backside. If Lex's dad was still around I think he could do it. Now about my Lex. I know he's got a mouth on him. I've had to slap it shut a few times myself, but he's just a baby. Then this Ob goes and says those things about him. Then he calls me a budinski. I have it in mind to find Lex's dad and have him teach this Ob a real lesson. And what does Ob know about woodpiles anyway? It sure would be nice to have a man around the house at times like this to show blowhards like Ob just where their place is. I know I've let myself go a little bit, so if I lose a few pounds and have my neck and chin tucked some and dye my hair again, maybe Lex's dad would leave that tart he's with and come home where he belongs and where he could show Lex how to deal with the likes of Ob.

Goths

You know how people are always talking about doing the right thing to leave the world a better place for their children and grandchildren? They don't seem to mention great-grandchildren and I think I know why. Did the Goths feel that way about their offspring? Did the Huns feel the same way? And what did they do for their children? I wonder about that.

First you had the Ostrogoths come down and take over and have a swell time for a few hundred years. Then they sacked Rome and in turn were sacked in Rome by some Huns, I think. Maybe not. Before that, however, you had the Visigoths sacking Rome and other cities. It was quite apparent, to me at least, that this was not a particularly engaging time. Lots of sackings. Then you looked up and here are the Zeagoths bent on sacking Rome, not to mention the notorious sacking of Rome by the Miscegoths. Evidently, Gothdom and Romedom did not meet eye-to-eye.

That brings us to their great-grandchildren, those of the Goths and the Huns, that is.

Research I have just come across suggests we can pass on the roamings of the Huns for the very simple reason that they are not credited with any sacks of Rome. I was mistaken a minute ago. Now don't get me wrong, the Huns were first-rate sackers and they have a glowing record of city-sackings. The fact is the evidence shows they didn't get quite as far as Rome. If they had they undoubtedly would have sacked Rome in a thorough and professional manner.

Let's say you are part of the horde that has just sacked a city, say Rome. You've had your bath, something to eat and a nice lie-down. Naturally, your thoughts now turn to starting a family. You want Goth progeny. Your children and their children, your grandchildren, are just diamonds in the rough. (And you don't have to change their loin cloths.) Great-grandchildren? They are not really the lights of your life because you are not likely to ever see them.

You didn't start your family at a young age. Why? Because you have been busy moving with the horde sacking cities and expanding the Gothic empire. This is about 600 A.D., so travel was not swift. You couldn't punch up your Uber app, for example. What's even more relevant is the life expectancy of a Goth in 600 A.D. was around 34 for a male if he avoided fatty foods and didn't fall prey to the tobacco habit.

We have reached a point here where we can safely say that the question of doing the right things to leave the world a better place for their great-grandchildren is answered by saying great-grandchildren were not on the radar for these Goths.

Once I had to fill in a job application asking for my ethnic heritage. It was even after employment rules were "modernized." I found the question not only unnecessarily invasive, but also insulting. My bloodline was not going to be a factor in my job performance. I put down that I was Goth-American. I was not called in for an interview.

Flight From Hell

Have I told you about my Flight From Hell? No? It was a flight on an airplane one is not likely to forget soon. I certainly won't forget. The memory is burned into my, well, my memory. Did I say "a flight on an airplane"? That's redundant, isn't it? It's a little embarrassing for a writer to fall into that trap. I'm not going to change it, though, because it reads just fine. So sue me.

When you've been through a Flight From Hell, *on an airplane*, you are going to have times when you are testy. I have them. I'm having one now. You weren't there so you don't know how terrifying the flight *on the airplane* really was. Anyone reading this now who had a seat on that flight can back me up on this.

I got to the airport and checked in at the desk. I showed her my ticket and she started hammering away at the computer. I waited. Then I hit her with it. "I fly this airline a lot, so could I get upgraded to business or first?" I asked rather importantly. She looked up at me and said "no."

My seat was in the middle between an aisle seat and a window seat. I am not a big man so the middle seat is not uncomfortable for me. A seat in business or first would offer a lot more space, however, and I'm still peeved that the airlines don't give you a chance to upgrade. What's the big deal if there are empty seats up there? Whatever happened to the customer comes first?

After we took off and got up to cruising altitude, they served us a meal. It was nothing to write home about. What would you say? Dear Mother and Father, the fish was hot and the rice was okay. I got a cookie too. See? The passengers sitting next to me, one on the aisle and one at the window, didn't have much to say. I didn't say much either.

About half way through the flight things got a little bumpy. I don't like bumpy, I like smooth. The pilot reminded us to fasten our seat belts. I don't like that either. It shows us that the pilot doesn't like bumpy himself. Then it got bumpier. Did I tell you I had the fish and the rice? And that I don't like bumpy? The pilot said everybody should return to their seats. I looked around and took note of the fact that no one was out walking.

When it got real bumpy there were some shouts from some of the passengers. The ones who really didn't like bumpy is how I figured it. Later, after we'd landed, some of the passengers said I was crying like a baby, you know, shrill and all. Not true. I did exclaim a few times. It was bumpy, remember, but I was not "crying."

I guess the worst part was when I went grabbing for the sick bag and didn't get it open in time. The passengers on my left and on my right said it was the worst part of the flight for them as well. The stewardesses? They were no help at all. They should show you how to open those sick bags as part of the instructions they give at the start of the flight. I'll bet you'll need a sick bag a lot more often than you'll need a life jacket.

We land. I get off the plane. I go in and clean up. I go to baggage claim. No bag. Great! I wait. No bag. Everyone else has grabbed their bags and are on their way home. I ask someone where my bag is. "What flight were you on, sir?" I tell him. "Well, sir, your bag would be over there on that other carousel, just as we announced. Is that your bag right there, sir?" Well, yes. It was still the Flight From Hell, I can tell you.

The Unicorn And The Mermaid

A unicorn and a mermaid walk into a bar. I was there so I can vouch for the events and conversations that follow. "What'll ya have?" asks the bartender. "We need directions," one of them says. "To where?" "To Noah's Ark." "Oh, that's that new bar over on the corner of Birch and John Streets." "That's not what it says in Genesis." "Perhaps. What do you want to go there for?" "To get on the Ark." "Why?" "Haven't you heard? The deluge." "The deluge?" "Yes, the deluge." "Oh, that. Well that boat sailed a long time ago." "Oh my."

"You're not from around these parts, are you?" the barman asked. "No." "Haven't seen anyone like you before if I remember correct. Where are you from?" "He's from Eden." "She's from Atlantis." "Where'er they?" "Eden's west of Nod." "Atlantis is south of...south of...south of everything, I'd say."

"You two are kinda strange. I don't mind having you here but when the afternoon crowd starts to build it could get rough for you." "Whatever do you mean?" "Let me put it this way. There's one regular who would look at the two of you and would want to saddle you up and ride you, one one way and one another way, if you get my drift." "No, I don't." "Neither do I." "Well, I warned you." "Thank you, you have been very helpful." "And very nice to us as well."

"What are you going to do now?" the barman asked. The unicorn said, "I'm going to open up a carousel franchising business." The mermaid said, "I'm going to secure animation and product merchandising rights to myself and form an LLC in Hollywood." "Good luck to both of you." "Thank you and the very same to you."

As the two turned around and started to walk away from the bar, the bartender stopped them. "Excuse me, but I have to ask. You are a unicorn, a small horse with a large horn growing out of your forehead." "Yes." "And you are a beautiful woman with lovely exposed breasts and a fish from the waist down." "Yes." "How do you..."

And just then in walks the "regular." "Uh-oh," gasps the bartender. "Holy hamhocks," shouts the regular. "What the hell is this?" he adds. Upon further examination he recognized that there was a unicorn and a mermaid in the bar. "Set me up," he shouts to the bartender, "and where's my saddle?" he shouts again. He evidently didn't just talk but rather he shouted things.

The unicorn and the mermaid stared at the regular. The regular looked at the unicorn and then at the mermaid. To the mermaid he shouted, "Come to papa, mama." As he shouted he headed toward the mermaid. His demeanor was lustful and no one would go away thinking otherwise. No one including the unicorn.

As the regular approached the mermaid reaching out, he shouted again, but it wasn't words. It was a kind of, well, a combination of whack and wonder. He had not got all the way to the mermaid. The unicorn, on the other hand, had got all the way to the regular – from behind – and had inserted himself into the unfolding scene.

The bartender and I could not restrain ourselves and laughed at the broad comedy of the burlesque we were watching. Later, when I had paid my bar tab and was getting up to leave, the bartender said, "Nobody's going to believe me when I tell them this story." I could not disagree.

Lunatists

When man first crawled out from the oceanic goo that covered Earth to make his claim at the forefront of the animal kingdom by dint of his superior intellect and his physical versatility, he stopped and cast his eye along the shoreline in a survey of his new-found domain. He reflected and then he said, "What was I thinking? Where are my manners?" He turned around politely and attentively and said, "Come on out, honey, I should have observed 'Ladies first'."

Whereupon a woman emerged, dripping of the same goo as the guy and wearing the look on her face that was unmistakable to the man then and would be for the next 14.5 billion years to the men who followed. She sidled up alongside the man. She spoke for a few minutes, he nodding his head from time to time. When she fell silent finally, he apologized.

Then it was time for business. Hours passed, the sun dropped toward the ground, the sky darkened and the moon, round and full, rose from the other direction. "Cool," the man said. "Lunatic," the woman half whispered. Neither, however, saw in the transpiring of their first day in the open air the potential significance in it. They were exhausted.

Who did see the significance was a couple who in our own times married in a civil ceremony in a "chapel" in a Las Vegas casino. (It could have been anywhere else, but it was in Vegas.) What they saw was a moonrise too, only it occurred to them that with a little imagination, a web site, a hashtag address, and a small initial investment, they could separate nascent believers from some cash.

This Ob-servation now takes a turn in direction that may disturb some readers, and I feel obliged to warn you, if you are among those readers, to proceed knowing that you are at risk of being offended by some unscrupulous undertakings. I can say that because I have it on good authority that these two behaved recklessly.

After a short honeymoon the pair went back home to their mobile home park in a state east of the Rocky Mountains where they quit their jobs, developed that web site and launched their "crusade." They averred that the moon was God. Once a month, or so, they preached, the moon rounded Earth as much as a guardian angel might watch over his, or her, charges, how a shepherd might tend to his, or her, flock. (The newlyweds apparently were not above extracting symbolisms from other religions.)

Inside of six months, Lunatism was the 13th largest religious denomination in the country. And the fifth fastest growing. The couple had sold their space in the trailer park and moved to a much more spacious place in the state capital. They also bought a beachfront house out in Malibu, California. A French real estate agent was scouring properties for them on the Riviera.

Lunatists praised the work the couple performed. Many Lunatists were comforted also by financially supporting certain select public office candidates who were of the same persuasions and who, in turn, praised Lunatists for their piety and patriotism and, we assume, their political sagacity and uncommon generosity. Backs were turned for mutual scratching.

Not much time passed. Not much at all. Then…

At the inevitable news conference, the gentleman of that same couple explained in heartrending detail, tears streaming down his face, how sorry he was when arrested in a motel room in that same state capital (he was not alone in the room.) The gentlelady of that same couple (she was not the one in the motel room with her husband) wore that look on her face that we talked about earlier in this Ob-servation which was, still, entirely unmistakable.

Any Old Port

Content enough with staying on land, most of us eschew piloting airplanes or sailing tall ships. Statistics support me on this. Any attempts to refute me will come to nothing. Common sense is an even more convincing ally in my argument, so who among us will be so impolitic to, you know, go vs. common sense?

Take sailors. They're sailing along, these sailors, and a roiling sea tells them something. It tells them there's a storm a-brewing. Common sense doesn't tell them a storm is a-brewing. They know all about a-brewing storms from experience. Sailors, oceans, storms. They go hand in hand, or, rather, hand in hand in hand. Experience.

No, common sense tells them to land the dang airplane. Airplanes are hearty machines, but storms can...oops, they're sailors so common sense tells them to go alee. Their "Sailors Handbook of Common Sense Aphorisms and Other Learned Lessons of Life on the High Seas" tells them to put into any old port in a storm.

Sounds simple, doesn't it? There is rain, lightning, thunder, wind, choppy waters, cries of despair, abandoned hope. The captain, taking charge, calls for the ship's charts. He pulls them from the waterproof cylinders, rolls them open, calls for his sextant, a glass of rum, and begins to read where his ship is situated and where the closest "any old port" is.

There!

Sounds simple, doesn't it? Well, Captain Smarty Pants, you are in for a real surprise. That port you found in hopes of docking in a calmer clime is run by a bureaucrat who not only got passed over recently for a promotion to the head office, but also his sister arrived unannounced two days ago with twice as much luggage as usual. And her four brats.

"What do you want?" the bureaucrat inquired of the boat's captain.

"We are sailors who need a port in a storm."

"Why's that my problem?"

"Allow me to re-phrase: we are sailors who need *any* old port in a storm."

"Name."

"What?"

"Name."

"Why do you want my name?"

"To see that it matches your passport."

"Passport?"

"Yes, and your visa?"

"Visa?

"Yes. Have you had your shots?"

"Now just a darn minute. There's a big storm out there. You have to let us take refuge in your port. It is one of the sacred covenants of the sea."

"Oh, yeah, says who?"

"Everybody says, that's who."

"You got a permission slip?"

"This is whale dung. I'll have you up on charges."

"Charges? How about I call some people I know and have them come over and confiscate your treasure and sink your boat?"

Anyway, the two they talked like this for a long time only to come to find out the bureaucrat was overstepping his bounds. It was true that maritime convention provided for safe harboring for any vessel in distress or approaching distress. The bureaucrat's enquiries about passports, visas, shots and the like were not defensible and, as it turns out, his sister was really getting on his nerves. And those bratty kids.

The captain returned to his boat a bit shaken. He had not ever been interrogated so impudently about taking refuge in any old port in a storm before, nor had he ever heard of any other captains being so ill-treated. As he related this to his crew and ordered them to make ready to sail into the safety of this old port's dockage, a sleek Chris-Craft swooped in suddenly and one of the bureaucrat's friends he spoke of earlier fired warning shots across the captain's bow before boarding parties went on to steal all they could from the boat. The captain was mortified. The landside bureaucrat watched from his office window.

There is no moral to this story. This is not Aesop. I think you know how I feel about Aesop. If not, you will.

Mousetrap

You have, I am going to assert, heard the old adage that if you build a better mousetrap the world will beat a path to your door. Based on this statement, you might expect there is pent-up demand. Must be a lot of mice on the loose and the current model on the market to grab the innocent little quadrupeds must not be doing the job. Nevertheless, there is not yet a "better mousetrap" and there hasn't been a contender since before Eric the Red set sail. Adagists persist in this unproductive call for an improved mechanism and nothing gets done. That is disturbing. Is it possible, just maybe, that the cheese-tempting, snap-over mousetrap is the best we can do?

That's just one question. There are others. Is it the cheese? Have the mouse hunters ever stopped to market test which cheese was the one most certain to lure the timid little furry rodent to his death? A trip to any delicatessen will confirm that different cheeses smell differently. I have seen a mouse and I can report that they have noses. The aroma of one cheese compared to the aroma of another suggests that a mouse will be more inclined toward one versus another.

Cats. Now, you say, we're getting somewhere. But wait, cats are reputed to be champion mousers, yet they play a very limited role in the extinction of mice. Lazy creatures that they are, cats cannot be held accountable solely for the overpopulation of rodents, but they should be made to take some share of the blame.

If the current mousetrap is still best for the job and the job is still not getting done, can we indict the mousetrap manufacturer on another score? I think so. Here's how: the last time I purchased a mousetrap the only thing I got was a mousetrap. Makes you wonder, doesn't it? Because when you last purchased a washing machine you didn't get just a washing machine. Along with it came an Operating Manual.

You put a sophisticated tool like a mousetrap into the hands of an inexperienced housewife, for example, and the hoped-for results might come down to nothing more than pure chance. I've told you about that bozo on my block who sabotaged our Neighborhood Watch efforts. Well, believe me, without access to a properly written Operating Manual, his wife would find her fingers in the mousetrap the first time she tried it. Which proves my point. I would feel a whole lot better if the mechanically challenged bozo's fingers were the ones in the trap. Except that he's not about to get up off his duff and do a man's job. What, didn't I tell you about him? Take my word for it that he is a bozo.

Why an Operating Manual? Because it would describe how to set up the trap. Using easy-to-follow instructions and drawings, it would show where the cheese should be placed. The consumer-friendly mousetrap manufacturer would also include a small scale so that the proper amount of cheese is weighed before attaching it to the gizmo on the trap. I am sure that the U.S. Department of Agriculture also has a recommended portion of cheese depending upon the species and typical size of rodents in your region of the country. Not to mention how to fold back the snapper and lock it correctly so that it is ready to spring upon the dreaded creature.

Where to place your mousetrap(s) may be more important than any other procedure in the War on Mice. The Operating Manual would describe the favorite locations for mice. It wouldn't surprise me if one of those is your kitchen. Kitchens are where you keep your food unless you have a separate pantry. If you do, put a mousetrap in your separate pantry even if the Operating Manual fails to mention that.

Now you families with toddlers and crawlers will need to take special precautions as to the placement of your mousetrap(s). This is to avoid any mishaps involving your youngsters' fingers, toes or tongues. This you will have to do on your own, for I am willing to wager that the lawyers at the mousetrap manufacturers concluded that any mention in the Operating Manual of potential hazards to children is just too incendiary and is better left unsaid and unwritten. Lawyers, you gotta love 'em!

It Rained

When someone says, "It rained yesterday," no one ever asks what was the "it" that rained. So, as usual, it is left again to these Ob-servations to go where others are fretful to go. We will ask: what was the "it" that rained?

Was it the sky? No, the sky cannot rain as the sky is no more than the empty space above our heads. Was it the clouds? Some may say so thinking that clouds are large containers of water. They aren't. Haven't they ever attended school? Come on. Was it the accumulation of numerous hydrogen molecules interacting with half as many oxygen molecules? This is more likely. I think we've answered that. H-2-O, remember?

Now we have a real poser. When someone says, "It rained a half inch yesterday," no one ever asks how it was determined to be a half inch. People cannot go about throwing out answers like that with no substantiation. "Oh, the weatherman said so." Stuff and nonsense, I say. I say the weatherman ought to be made to prove it when he says it rained a half inch yesterday.

From what I have seen of weathermen they'd have a hard time proving that anything happened yesterday. They shouldn't take this personally. On the contrary, I am willing to say that weathermen would be a fun bunch of fellows to have lunch with. I just like proof.

I went on the Internet to check it out but that got me nowhere. I'm beginning to have doubts about this Internet thing. My encyclopedia set is about 25 years old. That was no help at all. Then it hit me like a thunderclap. Do what Horace Greeley said, "Go to the source." A few phone calls and I had "my man." More properly, I had my woman. She was a Teaching Assistant in the Science Department at a nearby university.

"How do you measure rain?" I started, not wanting to waste time.

"Who is this?" she responded.

"Constantinople Ob."

"That's your name?"

"Yes, it is."

"What kind of a name is that anyway?"

"Oh, it's just my name."

"You should change it."

"Why?"

"Never mind, what do you want?"

"To find out how you measure rain?"

"Why?"

"I'm writing an Ob-servation."

"Is this some kind of prank call?"

"No." (Followed by an explanation of my Ob-servations and this particular topic.)

"We use a rain gauge."

"How?"

"How what?"

"I mean how does it work."

"I don't know, it just does."

This was not getting me anywhere. I explained about the weatherman and the claim of a half inch of rain yesterday.

"Why don't you ask him?"

"Who, the weatherman?"

"Who do you think we're talking about?"

"He didn't measure the rain. He just reported it."

"Did you ask him?"

"Well, no, I didn't."

"Instead you called here to ask me. You don't sound too tightly wrapped."

"No reason to make this personal. I assumed that your institution would have the answer and you would help me."

"You assumed wrong. Why don't you go on the Internet? There's lots of stuff there." I expressed my disappointment about my futile search on the Internet. "My other line is ringing," she said before I finished my explanation about the Internet, "I have to go," she said hanging up.

I had lots to think about after this conversation, one of which was I now think Horace Greeley misspoke.

New Number One

Of God's several mistakes, or "quality escapes" as I've heard them called, made during the 6-day creation week, I always maintained that pigeons and termites were chief among them. A persuasive case can be made for both. Take termites. What a stupid existence. Eat wood (somebody's house, for instance) then die in a gas attack when the property sells and a fumigation tenting is mandated. Pigeons, too. If you do not believe me, just look at what they do to statues and from light poles. Just disgusting.

Reflection on this topic now brings me to a new number one. It is the flea. Its only claim to fame is that it can jump up the equivalent of 160 times its own body height. Apart from this trait (and here we all have to sing in chorus, "whoopdi freakin do" to that) the flea bites animals for a sip of nutrition then goes into hiding. The angels on God's design staff who drafted this one must have spent the morning nursing hangovers.

Much has been written about the flea, pejoratively and uncomplimentary, but only because the flea is a stinking useless irritating parasite with no possible reason for existing except maybe in some gruesome twist in the progress of nature to bite me repeatedly during flea season.

Scientists estimate that more than five hundred thousand animal species have gone into extinction since Adam and Eve sprayed DDT around the edges of Eden way back in time to give the extinction process a good head start. I estimate it is more than six hundred thousand. Five hundred thousand, six hundred thousand, there's plenty enough room either way for me to question why the flea is not one of them.

Then someone comes along and argues that all God's creatures have a purpose and that the flea is part of the food chain providing nourishment to some other animal. Well gag me with a spoon! Any animal with fleas on its menu ought itself be a victim of extinction and the sooner the better.

I bring up flea bites because my experience with them has been pretty unpleasant. For some reason – and I wish science had an answer for this one – fleas are especially fond of me, whereas I have talked to plenty of people who are not at all affected by them. These people have a bevy of dogs at home and nothing, no bites. My ankles are blotched from the dirty little things.

What then can be done about fleas? These so-called scientists have failed to step forward with any ideas. I am sure that if I were holed up in an ivory tower laboratory I would be bereft of practical ideas as well. I am not. Not bereft. How about this? How about we address the problem at its source? Where's that you ask. Dogs. It's where fleas live and do whatever it is they do. I do not advocate the elimination of dogs. That would take weeks. Oh, and it would be wrong, I guess.

I propose a "Flea Bath Holiday." At the same time on the same day every dog owner dips his or her dog into a flea bath. Sometime in April sounds about right to me just before flea season opens officially. They tell me that flea baths kill fleas. End of discussion.

Cats are different. They get fleas, too, only you can manage them easier by giving them a wide berth. Stay away from them. They don't like soapy baths. I learned that about cats when I ran the cat obedience school I told you about. I did. In another Ob-servation. The one entitled "Obedience." Well, say what you will, I did tell you about it. I sometimes think your memory is failing.

Regardless. I tried the cat bath lesson one time at my obedience school. I think I learned more than the cat did. I would have tried it a second time, but I would have needed to wear those big heavy protective gloves that went up above my elbows to minimize the scratching. Couldn't give a good bath wearing those.

My doctor, and here I think he was trying to be funny, advised that I wear shoes that are taller than 160 times the height of the common household flea. He asked me if I wanted him to write a prescription for flea-protective footwear. I declined. I don't think my insurance will pay for that one. As I was leaving, the receptionist told me they don't validate parking any longer.

Tontine

Two guys walk into a tavern. They stand just inside the door looking around. As their eyes adjust to less light they walk over to the bar but they don't take stools. They stand. "Gotta booth?" one of them asks the barkeeper. "Yeah, we got booths." "Which one?" "Which one what?" "Which one can we sit in?" "Take your pick." "Okay." They order two drinks.

I'm sitting in a booth eating a sandwich and having a diet soda. I'll follow lunch with a glass of beer and then a snifter of cognac. When I have finished I'll go home and have a nap. I like naps.

The two guys – their eyes apparently fully adjusted to their new sur-roundings – take the booth next to mine. I think nothing of it, though there are other booths farther away and unoccupied. The bartender arrives a few moments later and puts down what appear to be dark ales and a dish of pea-nuts. I think about how most bars don't put out peanuts like they used to. I wonder if it's a cost-saving thing. That's what I was thinking.

I can hear the two guys. Either they haven't taken notice of me or they don't care that I can hear them. Guy A says, "A toast." Guy B says, "Absolutely." Guy A says, "Here's to Jimmy Lee, our dear and departed com-rade. He lived well and died in peace. May we have his fortunes." Guy B says, "Well said." They each drink to complete their toast to the dead guy.

Guy A says, "Well, you know what this means." Guy B says, "Of course." After a moment of silence, Guy A says, "How do you wanna do it?" Guy B says, "I'm not sure. I've thought about it, but I can't come up with the right thing to do." Guy A says, "Me neither." There's another silence. They sip their drinks. I go on with my sandwich.

"We could divvy up half and half," Guy A says, "even though that's not what we said." "Can't," Guy B says, "that's not what we said." "What we said scares the pee out of me," Guy A says. "Me too," Guy B agrees. "Just our luck," one of them says. I couldn't distinguish which one.

I finished my sandwich and soda and motioned for the bartender to bring me a beer. He did. "Something quick," Guy B says. "Oh, yeah," Guy A answers. "But what? Guns?" Guy B asks. My ears perked up. It was a development in the conversation that would perk anyone's ears. You don't hear discussions of guns in a bar without taking notice with some ear-perking.

"I don't own one," Guy A admits. "Either do I. We could buy a couple," Guy B counters. "I suppose. Ever do that?" Guy A queries. "No," Guy B says, "but it can't be hard. Seems everyone owns one these days." "Let's ask this guy," Guy A suggests. "Okay, can't hurt," Guy B says.

Two guys in a bar talking, one guy having lunch and a barkeep out back out of sight momentarily, meaning there's only four people in the tavern. By default, the "this guy" turns out to be me. "Excuse me," Guy A says, "do you have a minute?" I answer yes. "Thanks," he says, "my name is (whatever it was I didn't catch it. My ears were perked not for names but for "guns") and my friend's name is (didn't get that one either.)

They got up and joined me in my booth.

I introduced myself. "Constantinople? That's your name?" "Yes, Constantinople Ob." "Really? What kind of a name is that?" "Oh," I answered automatically, "it's just my name."

"Don't mean to disturb you," Guy A says, "but we are hoping you might know how we can buy a couple of guns. We need them." "A gun store, I guess," I tell them. "Is it easy?" he asks. "I don't know. I've never owned one myself," I admit. "Oh, then you probably wouldn't have any recommendation about what kind to buy." "No. It would probably depend on what you were going to do with them." "Naturally," Guy A said thoughtfully.

I sipped my beer. Not being a particularly bold person, I was surprised to hear myself ask, "What do you want to do with them?" "A duel," Guy B broke in. "We need to have a duel to complete a tontine." I was stunned into silence. I swallowed the rest of my beer. The barman saw us talking together and saw also my nod. He came over. "Ready for your cognac?" I said yes.

Guy A blurts, "A cognac. That sounds like a delightful idea. Make it three and put them on my tab." Perhaps out of respect for the impending service of cognac, more silence went on until the snifters arrived. Then Guy B says, "Perhaps we should explain." Guy A says, "That would be fair."

Guy B says, "We are the last two signatories to a tontine we created years ago with eight of our friends. As you know, with a tontine the last surviving participant receives all that is in the agreement." (I did not know that.) Guy A steps in to say, "Our tontine included a stipulation, however, which makes us face this painful development." Guy B says, "We decided back then that when time had taken all but two of us, those two had to duel to death so that the now lone survivor would – we hoped – have more time to enjoy the assets of the tontine." "This," Guy A added, "is what we agreed to. Now, you see, we feel we need to honor it."

I sipped my cognac. I wished I were a thousand miles away. "I am speechless," I said to the two guys. "It is unusual, I suppose," Guy B says. Guy A added, "Most tontines don't call for gunplay." (I did not know that either, but I was willing to make a guess at it.) "It doesn't have to be guns," Guy B volunteers, "only they seem like the most efficient way to do it. Quick and certain, you know." "If one of us shoots straight and first," Guy A advises. "Oh, yeah," Guy B agrees, "sure."

We all sipped at our cognacs. The barman walked over to see if he could bring anything else to the table. The consensus was no. He threw his towel over his shoulder and said, "I overheard what you said. You seem stymied." (Nods of agreement.) Why don't you flip a coin, winner take all? No guns to buy, no bodies to dispose of, no intrusions into your private life by the police." "That would dishonor our bond with our dead mates," Guy A said.

"We took oaths," Guy B revealed. The barman responded, "You place honor above expediency. Your pals would be proud. Let me ask this, can you be certain that you would not kill each other in a duel?"

The question hung in the air. We all sipped at our cognacs. The barman went on. "It's a very possible outcome. It would be a very unsatisfactory way to play out your tontine. The honor to your dead mates would evaporate in a flash. The assets would go unclaimed for a period of years and then be turned over to the state which would fritter them away. Your families, such as you may have, might sue for the proceeds, but they would soon discover that tontines are illegal (I did not know that) and they would have no standing to recover the assets."

We all sipped at our cognacs.

Guy A said, "What do you mean, tontines are illegal?" "The statement speaks for itself." "But it's our stuff," Guy B claims. "The state will have a contrary opinion as well as the force of law," the barman corrected him. "They can't do that, can they?" Guy A asked, not fully expecting an answer he'd like. The barman shrugged his shoulders. "Oh, merde," Guy B spat.

We all sipped at our cognacs.

"Are you a lawyer?" Guy B asked the barman.

"No, I'm an actor. This is my second job," he said.

"Now what?" Guy A asked. No one answered.

The barman said, "How about another round on me?"

The consensus was yes.

Get Your Goat

There's always someone, whether it's the guy in the house across the street, or the one in the apartment across the common area, or that buzzard in the last house in the cul-de-sac, or the fellow in the cell block just above, or that bearded bird who lives in the RV in the grocery store parking lot, there's always one it seems.

Who you won't go out your door when he's outside. He just looks like he's itching to get your goat. And there is no one I know who wants to get his goat got.

They have a look in their eyes, these guys. They're just begging for trouble. I don't know why. Oh, it's not just trouble they are looking for. No. Also, they are always "right." Gad, that can be annoying. No matter what you say to them they have a correction or an opposing opinion or a scoffing to answer you. They are always out to get someone's goat. If they had a den where they lived, they'd have goat's heads mounted on the walls.

I know you want to know and I will tell you, but if I do you will find it near impossible to get to sleep tonight for the blood-chilling, heart-racing bracing this tale will tell. Easy on there, Ob, that may have been a bit exaggerated. You get the idea, though, don't you? This all sounds familiar, doesn't it?

For me it was a guy who lived a few doors up the street. He was a man of colossal indifference when it came to social intercourse. He once said it himself. He said, "I am not ashamed to admit it, I do not like people." And then, it is reliably reported I believe, he added, "generally." In the warm months he appears outdoors without a shirt on.

About him it can be said he was a man of no principles. Well, of low principles at any rate. Any higher principles for him than low would be a roofish reach. On a scale of principles from low up to high or just plain elevated, he would settle at the low end. You know what, we're drifting to the side here. More correctly, I am drifting. Back to the point.

It happened that one morning when I looked out my window, a practice I undertook to ward off interacting with the guy I was going to tell you about, I saw that the paperboy had left my paper in the gutter. (That juvenile delinquent nephew of mine sometimes substitutes for my regular paperboy and I have suspicions he was on duty that morning.)

Upset at Oliver Ovid Ob, for that is my nephew's name, and otherwise inattentive, I am out the door to get my soggy paper. Then I hear, "Hey, Ob." That from the guy who I was going to tell you about. "Curses," I say to myself. "Oh, good morning," I say to him. I step up my pace to retrieve the paper and get quickly back into my house when I feel the crosshairs on my back and in the middle is me as goat.

"No, it isn't," he replies. I have no one to blame (other than my miscreant nephew) but myself. I should have scanned the street from my window to be sure he wasn't there, and, if he were, to stay inside.

So far it's been "Hey, Ob," "Oh, good morning," and "No, it isn't." I look up into a pleasant cloudless sky with morning colors dancing above me and feel a refreshing air on my arms. "Why isn't it?" I ask myself.

"Because there's nothing good about it," he says. (Had I said that other thing out loud?) "Wha..?" is all I can get out before he lays in. "Have you seen the news?" he shouts. By answer I hold up my waterlogged daily newspaper. "Hell, man," he shouts again, "stay in touch with things if you want to know what's going on. It's all over the Internet and TV. What's wrong with you?" Nothing as far as I can ascertain, but I don't answer, for he has started in with a description of why there is something wrong with me. I can feel my goat getting got.

"It's people like you who are to blame." (I don't remember what he said from then on until I heard) "new taxes." "Wha...?"

"Hell, man, you..." (again words he said and words I don't remember until I heard) "...inside your place so's I can set you straight about this problem. I've got principles I live by and I'm going to have to instill them in you if it takes all day. You got a pot of coffee going? I like mine strong." I was about to say that I will take mine with arsenic when I heard him say, "You got any donuts, too?"

There's always someone out there goat getting.

Where I've Been

Maybe you noticed that there have been no new postings on this blog for some time. I hope so. I mean I hope you noticed. That would mean you are paying attention. Perhaps you were even expectant. The truth of the matter is that I got involved in some, hmmm, what should I call them, okay, things. Things not directly associated with my Ob-servations. I do have a life outside this blog after all.

The first thing is you probably don't think that I think about politics too much because I don't get into that arena in my writings. I thought so. But I do. People are always saying to me, "Ob, if you want to complain so much about politics, why don't you do something about it?" So I did. I ran for office. Not a big one, one of those local ones.

Let me tell you something about running for office. It's hard. I started about a year ago. Then right away the Christmas season came along and no one seemed to care about "local politics." I was going to resume the campaign in January when I got a phone call from Madrid Marriott. As you may remember, Madrid is a volatile character. In some situations her volatility can get the best of her. In this case, she said in the phone call, the other guy swung first. She put him in the hospital. ("He'll be all right," she assured me, "he can see out of the other eye.")

The phone call was from the police station. I had to go down there because John T. said he was going out of town again. "Business," he claimed. The desk sergeant didn't know who I was inquiring about until he read the arrest report. "Oh, her," he remarked. I told him that she told me that it was self-defense. "Not what it says here, bud," he responded. "She said there's a bunch of witnesses," I told him. "What, her drunk friends?" "Drunk?" "Oh, yeah."

Well, what with bail, lawyering up, interviewing "witnesses," a couple of appearances in court, hand-holding, doing what I could to support Madrid, I lost a lot of time when I should have been on the campaign trail. I was running for office. Madrid got off. There were unexplained discrepancies in that police report the desk sergeant had on file. The guy got out of hospital, too. He went to therapy for around eight weeks. Madrid, bless her heart, promised to behave.

Irony of ironies, I got called to jury duty. Prospective public servants are not excused from jury service where I live. Wouldn't that have been funny, too, if Madrid had to go to trial and I was called to be on her jury? Anyway, I got on a case. We let the guy off. He claimed it was self-defense. "The other guy swung first," his attorney asserted. Witnesses seemed to remember it that way also.

Time for campaigning for that local office just evaporated. I sensed I was losing ground. When I told Madrid about how hard it was to find time to campaign for reasons such as jury duty, she said, "What was the defendant's name?" I remembered it and told her. She laughed from here to Wednesday.

"He's one of my drinking buddies," she explained. When she said drinking she did that funny quotes thing with her fingers.

The last week or two before election day was a whirlwind of meeting and greeting; hectic mornings saying hello to coffee drinkers at local restaurants; calorie-laden lunches with fellows at construction sites; hand shaking at the evening meetings of Rotarians, Elks, Moose and (I thought mistakenly) Tigers (they are "Lions"); and phone calls in between.

The outcome might have been different if (1) I was not so fatigued and easily distracted from the non-stop pace and (2) the newscast with me in it hadn't been on television just a day before voting. You see, I was pretty out of it and when I said to a nice young lady can I kiss your baby (a time-honored campaign tactic, so I had heard) I leaned in a bit awkwardly before she could say no. I didn't realize that she was nursing that very baby at that very moment. As I said, I was pretty tired and my focus was not as sharp as usual. The episode was, however, in full focus on TV. My vote total prevented me from qualifying for a run-off for the office.

Cue Sharpening

It was a dark and stormy night and the bulbs over the tables cast their wavering shadows which made things shaky. As I stood sharpening my cue, I thought of the dimness, the darkness, the storm. (It was a dark and stormy night, remember.) Someone approached, someone I did not know nor had ever seen before nor, I assumed, would ever see again. He stopped, appeared to take in my cue sharpening technique, and said in a gravelly voice no doubt tempered by the now-well-known effects of the sot weed we all disdain today, "Got a match?" I looked him up and down and wondered why he should ask such a question, but instead I answered straightaway, "Yeah, my face and your butt."

It remained dark and the storm would not abate. "Huh?" he said in return. Huh what, I thought to myself. My face, your butt. Oops. The image of the Mr. Spooner of verbal slips came rushing toward me. I recovered. "No, no, my ass and your face," I corrected. (Darn it.) I tried to laugh it off.

"What's your problem, pal? All I did was ask for a match," he said not apologetically.

"My problem is you and if you have a problem it's me, so mystery solved," I countered.

"Huh?" (Again with the huh; where'd he come up with that one?)

By now my cue was sharper than it might ever be, a knight's lance on the threshold of another scheduled combat. "What a ditz," the gravelly voiced smoker murmured as he turned to another to seek the flame of his destruction.

Myself, I turned to the table, the light above swaying in rhythm with the winds of the storm (see above about storm and dark) motioning the shadows across the balls orchestrated in a triangle waiting the explosive break to form the onset of the game. (Pool, by the way, if you hadn't figured that out.)

I leaned in over the edge of the table, feet foundation supporting my crouching setup, arm on the verdant felt fabric that forms the field of action, opposite arm pendulumming the cue stick readying for the violence about to captivate the several onlookers who had silently moved in to bear witness to the event.

Out and back in, out and back in repeated as my corrected vision aligned the length of the cue to the cue ball on line with the yellow ball, out and back in... and then with a suddenness that always excites the crowd a heaving of the stick.

"What the..." The pointy part of the stick slipped right across the cue ball and it (the cue ball) skittered half-heartedly off to the left. The yellow ball remained unhurt, unfazed, unmoved. After a short burst of laughs, one of the onlookers cleared his throat and said, "What a ditz." It was not the same gravelly voiced fellow who coined the phrase earlier. "What in dog's name are you doing with a pointy cue stick? Are you bonkers or something?" someone asked out.

My friend, I tried to explain, without using any names or physical descriptions, warned me to "sharpen my cue" in advance of our big challenge match. "So I did," I added.

"Your friend is a moron and you are an imbecile. Now get the hell out of this billiards parlor and don't come back." I stepped outside. Had the night not been so dark and stormy, as I have reported to you, I could have seen what lay ahead thus avoiding the misfortunes embodied in the sign, "Slippery When Wet." It was both. I went down hard right there. Then I discarded that felonious cue stick now in two pieces after it collided with the cement.

Lost Tribes

Let the record show that every 30 to 40 years anthropologists find a new lost tribe in a jungle someplace, or so it seems. If these anthropologist whizzes are intent on beefing up their discovery batting average for "lost" tribes, they have been looking in the wrong places. I can show them geography where there are loads of "lost" tribes. It all depends on what you mean by "lost." More like what I mean by "lost." And "tribes," too.

Take, as just one example, that paint-peeling duplex over on Desert Edge Blvd. behind the midget auto racetrack. I'm not even an anthropologist and I'll lay three to one the people who live in the unit in back are "lost" by any definition, mostly the part that says "go away and leave us alone."

When I drive out to watch the races I don't pay the $5.50 to park in the track's parking lot. I find a place on a nearby street. The only thing it has cost me is a set of hubcaps one time. (I am not convinced that I cannot lay that prank at my disreputable nephew's feet.)

I've seen this duplex with my own eyes. The door is always closed, the blinds drawn, the curtains pulled across the windows, Thai restaurant menu flyers accumulating on the porch, and there is a television antenna on the roof, even in this digital age. That's not a jungle, you say? Fie on that, I say. There's no rule that says a tribe that's lost has to live in a jungle when they can rent a two bedroom, one bath duplex and find all the solitary confinement they could desire.

What could be the turning point to chalk these people up as a lost tribe would be a visit by one of these anthropologists.

Knock-knock. "Hello, anybody in there?" Knock-knock. "Hello." (Louder.)

Ding-dong, ding-dong. "Hello."

Knock-knock, ding-dong. "Hello." (Real loud.) My name is Mudd. Well, Dr. Mudd. I am an anthropologist. I'm here to discover you. Don't be afraid, I have no camera with me this time. Just a get-acquainted visit."

Ding-dong. "Anybody in there?"

The anthropologist is not getting aggravated, but I believe he is likely to run short of patience. He is an anthropologist who deals with observable facts. The residents of this duplex unit are not observable, (Nobody came to the door, remember?) so what other possible conclusion is there except that the "tribe" inside is of the "lost" variety?

The proof is in the pudding. (What does that mean, anyway?)

Dido Did It

So I'm doing a crossword puzzle the other day and the clue is, "Legendary founder of Carthage." Four letters. Ends in o…if I correctly spelt the other word. Leno? Fido? Bevo? Dido? Dido! Yes. (Okay, I confess, the answer is in the back of the book and I looked it up.) But doesn't that raise a big question? It did for me.

Dido is clopping along on the topside of an ass or a mule or a camel wondering how her day is going to be spent. Hungry or thirsty or just plain tired, maybe bored, she stops, dismounts and looks around. Not much to see. Sand, rocks, dust. She's about ready to remount the ass or the mule or the camel when she says, "Enough already. I'm staying here. I'll make this place a great metropolis." And wham! she founds Carthage. You go, girl, she tells herself.

Oh, the question I said it raises. If Dido can pound a stake in the sand and tie a little cloth on it attesting to the fact that travelers are now in Carthage, why can't I found a city? I have a stake and a hammer and I can probably find a piece of cloth. Then I wondered if Romulus and Remus used a stake and a piece of flagging in old Italia. Not important now. I don't own an ass or a mule or a camel, so I got in my car and drove out of town on a highway to an unpopulated part of the state. Can't found a city inside a city that's already founded is what I determined before I set off on my historic trip.

When I reached a likely spot – Didonian I called it with a little squeal of mirth – I went to the trunk of the car and got out the stake, a hammer, a slip of cloth and a stapler. I had pulled the car to a careful distance off the highway lanes even though there was barely any traffic. Safety first. With the metropolis-founding equipment in hand, I walked a few paces into the undeveloped terrain and pounded in the stake. And wham! I founded – get this – Constantinopolis. I finished the official act with cloth and stapler: click-click. There, that's done. Carthage was what, about 30 or 40 centuries ago? Whatever it was, it is different now. I don't know if you can get there from here.

Well anyway, I had a new city developing when up behind my own car pulls a second car – state trooper, highway patrol, ranger, I don't know. Hadn't seen that type of patrol vehicle before this. Whoop, whoop, whoop goes his "I'm-more-important-than-you" siren system. Something about his bearing, his attitude, his smirk, his swagger now that he's out of his car looking at me says he is not here to register as the first citizen of Constantinopolis.

"Good afternoon," he does not say. Instead he begins with, "Whater ya doing?" From that tone I can feel myself slipping between a rock and a hard place. Lying to a cop – is he really a cop, I ask myself as I study the uniform he's wearing – is bad form. Therefore I tell him the truth. I should have lied. I should have said I buried my pet parakeet under the stake as an honorific of returning the poor dead bird to the uncaged world from whence he came. Which itself would have been a lie because the parakeets I've ever seen always came from pet stores, from cages in pet stores. But I didn't lie. I told him I had just founded Constantinopolis in the Didonian tradition of Carthage and Rome and who knows what other great cities sprang from flags on stakes.

His bearing, his attitude, his smirk, his swagger, they all multiplied as he listened to the mission I was carrying out this day. I'll give him one thing. He did display some patience. He did listen to my explanation. However, when I had finished and smiled with satisfaction that I was the founder of a new city…and not a liar…he looked at me and said, "You on drugs, you been doing drugs today?"

I don't do drugs and was about to tell him exactly that when he blurted, "Hey, you some kinda straight-jacket mental case?" I'm not a mental patient and was about to tell him that when he asked, "Do you know where you are?"

I knew precisely where I was. I was at the geographical center of Constantinopolis, newly established right under my feet. And right under his feet, too, if he took the time and paid attention. The look on his face told me that was not the answer he would have expected from me, so I said, "What do you mean?" I was trying to buy time. For reasons I cannot account for, this officer, or whatever he was, had taken a dislike to me. When I asked him what did he mean, he shook his head in obvious disgust. I'll tell you what he said, leaving out the very disagreeable terms he used at and about me.

He said, "You are on federal land. You are in a national forest. You can't just come in here and start driving poles into the ground. There are rules. Don't you follow rules? What's more, we don't like druggies like you using federal land to do drugs on. We have laws against that. And what is this about founding a city? If I wasn't going off shift in 30 minutes, I'd run you in on all kinda charges. But I won't. I have a dinner date. With a sane person. Founding a new city! You are really bonkers, so piss off."

With that he pointed in the opposite direction my car was facing on the assumption, I assumed, he thought that was where I had come from. It struck me quickly that today I was not to be founder of a new city.

I began to trudge off when he yelled at me, "Hey, take your stupid pole. Don't think you can leave your trash here." I went back to pull up the stake, but he beat me to it. He pulled it out, looked at it, looked at me, then broke it in two over his knee. Bearing, attitude, smirk, swagger all were there in that moment on his face as he handed me the two pieces. I went to the trunk of my car and returned the city-founding devices. Dido, today, I was not.

The Nephew Episodes

(John Thom writes:)
I have now met the nephew of whom C. Ob has written a few times. That is, C. Ob has written about the nephew a few times and I have met him now. That nephew. A less appealing little jerk you cannot expect to encounter. I still believe he's the one who let the air out of the tires on my R.V. the night before I was set to head to the Ozarks. But I digress, don't I? The following Ob-servations in this section have in common that pestilent kin of Con's.

Nephew

They say that blood is thicker than water. What they should have said is that my nephew makes my blood run cold. I've just had it with him. Proper decorum prevents me from using very abusive language about him.

Let me tell you what he said at a family get-together. A bunch of his older relatives were standing around reminiscing and having a good time. He, my nephew, was over at the serving table where a nice food spread was set out. He was stuffing his face as usual. One of us, I don't know who, called to him to come over and join us. Someone asked him if he was having a good time. "No," he groused. (Really, I think that none of us cared for the kid and his cocky attitude.) Then one of us said, "You should try a little harder." A few of us laughed at that.

"Am I related to all of you?" he asked us in general. We looked at each other and nodded, yes, he was. "That sucks, man," he volunteered. Why, someone asked him. He said, and this is what I was referring to, he said, "Am I going to be as ugly as you when I grow up?"

That was sad enough, yet there was another time he turned my stomach. My doorbell rang one night and I went to answer it. No one was there, but a small basket was on the porch with a baby all wrapped in a blanket. I presumed it was sleeping. I wasn't sure because I have had very limited experience with babies. You understand, don't you, that now I'm in a real panic? What am I supposed to do? I am looking this way and that. A baby. I sure didn't want a baby. One thing that flashed in my mind was how Moses I think it was who found that baby floating in the Nile in a basket. Uh, a baby in a basket floating in the Nile. There, that's clearer.

Flashed is right. Everything happened very instantaneously. When I collected myself I called a couple of friends I knew who had kids. Each one said the same thing. "Call the cops." All the time the baby is just lying there quiet as a mouse. Sleeping, I figured.

Just as I was about to dial the police, the doorbell rang again and I hurried to answer it. It was my nephew and a couple of his pals. "Hi," he said. "What's new?" They all got a big kick out of that. "Hey, what's that?" he said when he noticed the basket. "It's a ba..." is all I got out as he reached for the basket and pulled the child out. "Hey, guys, look. A little rugrat. Let's play catch." And they did. Two or three tosses and I see it's a doll. The little rotter. My nephew, I mean.

And that's not all. This may have been the worst of all; it's so hard to choose. He came to me one day, my nephew, and asked if he could borrow my BB gun. (I told you I had one, didn't I, in other Ob-servations?) He said he and his buddies wanted to do some target shooting. It sounded innocent enough to me and a little more constructive on his part compared to some of his past adventures. I loaned it to him and gave him a box of BBs and several bull's-eye targets. I also instructed him on how to load the gun and – here I was rather emphatic – I told him about gun safety.

About two hours later, as I was watering some shrubs in my front yard, a police car pulled up to my curb. "Brrrp-brrrp" went that now-familiar horn gadget they have in police cars. I had heard it before. I turned.

"You live here?" the officer driving the car called to me. I told him I did and that prompted him to command me to come over to his car. I turned off the water and walked over.

"This your kid?" he said, motioning to the back seat. My nephew was seated there with two other boys. "Not really, he's my nephew. That one is, not the others."

"Don't get smart with me," was his response. I don't know why because I wasn't getting "smart" with him or anybody. I don't know if you've guessed by now but the cop driving the car and I had a past.

"You're the troublemaker," was his next statement.

"What do you mean?" I said. By now I had recognized him too. I didn't like where this whole thing was likely to go.

"This is perfect," he said. "Is this your gun?

"Yes, it's a BB gun."

"You don't have to tell me what it is. I know what it is. I've been trained. Did I ask you to tell me what it is?"

"No."

"Did you give it to these children and tell them to shoot at me?"

"Gad, no, what makes you say that?"

"I'm asking the questions here. I told you not to get smart with me. How'd they get the gun then?"

"I gave it to them. They were going to play target practice."

"You said just now that you didn't give it to them. Which is it?"

"Oh, no, I loaned it to them."

"So you did give it to them."

"I loaned it."

"Getting smart again, hey? Well, we'll come back to that."

"Sorry."

"Do I look like a target to you? Does my police unit look like a target to you? Does my partner look like a target to you?" (In all frankness, his partner looked like someone who wanted to take a nap.)

I started to answer when he said to the back seat, "Get outta the car, you little assholes, and you better wise up. And you," he said to me, "I'm keeping this gun. It's evidence." I bet he went home and gave it to his nephew. A nephew who knows how to behave.

The Resume

Twice your correspondent has lived through extraordinary periods in his life. The one you know about, the time I lived "off the grid" as described in a slew of Ob-servations and other reports done up during that time and published in this volume. Enough said about that.

The other extraordinary period was a rough patch of unemployment with the typical nerve-racking job search agonies. I did all the things the experts recommend, including building a comprehensive *curriculum vitae*, or resume. I thought I was on my way to re-entering the ranks of the contributing workforce. The experts are not to blame, for they could not have known the depths to which my reptilian nephew would sink to pull off what he calls his practical jokes. In other words, my suspicions led me to the usual suspect. The little rat.

You know how your personal documents are stored in your computer? Mine are too under my name, but unfortunately not password protected at the time. So what does Oliver Ovid Ob do? He goes into my documents file and messes with my resume. I don't know how many hours I worked on that thing to portray my background and qualifications in a complimentary and forthright manner. I also do not know how many hours (minutes?) that felon re-worked it. The little rat. (Did I already say that?)

A month or two passed and no responses to my campaign with prospective employers. It was a head-scratching interval. Draft a targeted letter and include a resume folded into an envelope just like the experts advised. I guess I should have paid a shade more attention. What do the kids say, "my bad"? Only after a frustrating length of time did I think to review my resume. Perhaps I had gone awry in some small way.

"Small way" does not cover it. My address, as stated plainly on the page, is not 1600 Pennsylvania Avenue. Neither is my middle name Gertrude. (The evil hand of my nephew was beginning to reveal itself.) Under accomplishments I purportedly single-handedly altered the orbit of Halley's Comet and cured toe jam.

My work experience does not include two years inside the Central Intelligence Agency as a mole from Tasmania. Seasonal employment as an investment counselor for "rich, elderly and clueless widows" is also not correct. Apparently I graduated from a college in Mongolia with a degree in fly-swatting. My correct phone number does not reach a biker bar hangout called "The Devil's Altar."

I almost gagged when I read that my career objective was to "secure employment with a forward-looking, technology-based company led by ex-mob strong-arm goons who would not know a spreadsheet from a bed sheet where I could embezzle enough to buy a mid-size country in a tropical zone."

It was here that I set about redrafting the resume. This time I password protected it.

Teaching The Young

It was a day like any other except I was doing something we all do once or twice a year. Okay, I admit it, I am a regular guy. What I mean to say is that I do things that suggest I have a pretty regular pattern in my life. Yes, I am the same person who you will recognize from my other Ob-servations, you know, the ones where I'm way out there on the edge.

But that intrepid adventurer also has a side that helps to keep his life in good order. For instance, everyone needs to file an income tax report each year, even if we find plenty of ammunition to raise objections. Well, Constantinople Ob is no exception.

Interesting that I should use taxes to profile my regular side. Those four and a half years of give-and-take with the IRS and then my state's tax collectors might show a level of attention to detail a little below that of some of my fellow citizens. It all came out okay in the end because I was able to get them to admit that I didn't owe them as much as they said at first. The IRS supervisor who stepped in and tried to browbeat me into paying their claim in full bit off more than he could ch...

You know, it might be better to examine that regrettable episode in a separate Ob-servation. Remind me to do that later. I mean remind me later to do that.

What I was doing was re-alphabetizing my state map drawer in my desk. This isn't a compulsion or anything. It is a simple nod to efficiency. You are planning a trip or you are doing some geographical research or you are studying state capitals. You don't want to grab New Mexico when you really want New Hampshire. I have maps of all 48 states in a single drawer. I'm lucky, I guess, that they all fold up pretty much the same size. That way they all fit in an orderly manner. This comes in handy when you are in a hurry. Actually, when I am in a hurry.

Let me give you an example about my nephew. He is in middle school. He's what we can call an "average student." One of his teachers wasn't so generous about him at one of those parent-teacher meetings, and I can still hear his dad carrying on about that. "How can we make him average?" his dad said he asked the teacher. And the teacher is supposed to have answered, and right here I have to express some admiration about a teacher who could say something like this, he answered, "Tell him to study more."

I think I was going to give you an example of how proper alphabetizing of the maps can be a benefit when you need a snappy response to an enquiry.

My nephew came into the den one day and said he needed a map of the biggest state. So I smiled and went right to the T's. I got to Tennessee and then went one further and pulled out Texas and handed it to him.

He stared at me for a bit then tossed the map on the floor and muttered something like "doofus" and left the room. How's a kid like that going to learn and get up to average with an attitude like that, I ask you.

"Lost"

Later, after I learned who was responsible, I was not at all surprised. The rest of the neighborhood? That was different. They didn't know him the way I did. The way he could...hold on, let me tell you what happened.

The first signs appeared on a Saturday morning. Ordinarily, most people would take scant notice. You've seen them, I'm sure, and you probably, like most folks, express sympathy before moving on. Typically, the signs are for a cat or a dog. They're headed "Lost." The signs on this Saturday morning followed that pattern. With one big difference.

I'll reprint it here for you: "Lost. Family pet. 6 years old. Brown with mottled marks on back. 18 feet long. Boa constrictor. Last seen: Backyard on Elm Street. Reward: $500 if returned alive." There was a phone number. By Saturday afternoon the police and the local Animal Control people were patrolling the scene. Neighbors were shut in their homes with all doors and windows secured. There was no answer at the telephone number in the "Lost" notice. It turned out to be an innocent victim.

Two weeks on, another Saturday morning, another "Lost" notice posted on telephone poles and fences in the neighborhood: "Lost. Pet crocodile. 6 ½ feet long. Likes water. Answers to the name of 'Chompers'. Do not approach with any sudden moves. Last seen: Swimming pool at the park. Reward." There was a telephone number. It was of no use. This second notice brought out TV news vans and it made the evening news broadcast. Several of our neighbors were on TV being interviewed. The snake and the croc were not found and speculation was that they found their way into the storm drains and were out of the neighborhood.

Things got back to normal. Until three weeks later. This time it was: "Lost. Family pet. Stands 18 inches high, about 2 ½ feet long with brownish, blackish hair. Tasmanian devil. Name: 'Attila'. Wear thick gloves if approaching. Last seen: Lawn in front of Tinkerbell Pre-school. Reward." There was a telephone number. It too was a dead-end.

By now the neighborhood was receiving these notices with some skepticism. Only one police car and a fire truck responded. Animal Control was around for just a half day. They didn't set any traps this time. Traps set after the croc scare inadvertently killed four cats and three dogs. There is some very contentious civil litigation surrounding that.

Just after the start of the school year, another poster drew attention again. This one, I'm glad to say, had a different outcome. First, the poster: "Lost. Dozens of scorpions. Family pets in several aquariums turned over by pranksters. Extremely poisonous. Do not approach. Last seen: Everywhere. No reward." There was no telephone number this time.

For some reason, no one (including the cops) had bothered to look closely at the posters until now when one curious resident turned over one of the notices to find a name faintly smudged on the back side of what looked like a rough draft for a school project. The name deciphered: Oliver Ovid Ob. Yes. That name should be familiar to readers of these Ob-servations. "Ob." That's my name. The "Oliver Ovid" part is that insufferable nephew of mine. The long arm of authority was finally catching up to that goof ball.

Being A Woodsman

When I was younger and smaller I used to go out into the woods whenever the opportunity presented itself. Being a city boy, I didn't get the opportunity very often. When I did, I went. Consequently, I am not now, nor was I then, very experienced in the woods. What follows should not be held against me. It should be held against my nephew. You remember my nephew, the pencil-neck Oliver Ovid Ob.

He was off from school when they have that break in the spring and his class had scheduled a trip to the mountains. What a surprise when I learned that nobody who knew Oliver had volunteered to go along as chaperone. Read sarcasm into that. And, yes, I admit that it was my own foolishness to let me get talked into doing it. More like stupidity. But a chance to go into the woods tempted me.

I was ready though. I decided to lay down some rules of behavior. I laid them out for Oliver and a couple of his friends I suspected could use the lecture. I was pleased when they said "deal" when I asked, "Do we have a deal?" Off to a good start.

The boys slept in one cabin, the girls in another and the chaperones – none of whom I knew and none of whom knew, I later discovered, my nephew – in a third.

The next day after breakfast and an adult vs. kids volleyball match (my nose wasn't broken by the ball, but the swelling would have fooled you) that nephew of mine and his buddies announced they were going to go on a hike out into the woods. I asked if they had the camp counselor's permission. "Oh, sure," they said, and that makes me wonder if they teach honesty in the schools anymore.

I found a chair and tried to nap but the throbbing all around by dose bade it ingbossible. That's how I had to talk, "by dose bade it ingbossible." At least the bleeding had stopped. Enough of the gory details. I'll move on to what occurred. First, let me tell you volleyballs are harder than they look.

It was about two hours later. No sign of Oliver and his friends. The camp was quiet. Everyone off on scheduled fun things. So with my head tilted back just a little, which made my nose feel better and I could breathe with less difficulty, I set out to find the truants.

I found them down by where the lake spills over some rocks and logs to start a small creek. Oliver, his two buddies, and a...a... "whad's dat?" I asked as I approached, looking out of the bottom of my eyes. "It's a..." one of them started. "It's a raccoon," Oliver told me. I hadn't seen one up close before. It looked more like a teddy bear. It looked more like a teddy bear because it was a bear cub. The boys were teasing it unmercifully. "You should be gareful," I said, "you never know whad a animal will do in the wild. Even small ones lige dat." I may be inexperienced in the woods, but that much I was aware of.

As I got those last words out ("...ones lige dat") the boys broke running away at a good clip. I guessed they heeded my caution. I guessed wrong. It was the appearance of the bear cub's parent that prompted them to run. I did some reading after this confrontation and learned it is usually, if not always, the mother who shows up to wreak havoc on anyone or anything threatening her "young."

So now I was up a tree. Literally. My dose is beeding again and the throbbing has returned. The boys are long gone. The camp is well beyond shouting distance. I'm in the woods where I have little experience (I told you I was a city boy). So I'm up a tree, figuratively also. I do not know at this minute if bears can climb trees. Of the three of us there, me, mama bear and baby bear, I am the only one who is uninformed about that.

What do you do when you need help? What do you teach your children to do in an emergency? That's right, call 9-1-1. Fortunately, the camp had assigned temporary phones to the chaperones. So I called. Beep, beep-beep. Ring-ring. Ring-ring. Ring-ring. Ring-ring.

"Nine-one-one, what's your problem?" They record those things, 9-1-1 calls. Maybe it's for training purposes or maybe it's to take the tapes to court if there's a sticky situation. The recording of my call contains some comments that are not all shouts and tearful entreaties. For example, I said:

"I'b ub a tree and by dose is beeding again."

"You're breeding?"

"Do, I'm bleeding," I emphasized.

"Why are you bleeding? Where are you cut?"

"I god hid in by dose wid a bolleyball. Never bind aboud dat. Dere's a bear down dere."

"You were playing ball in a tree? Are your friends there to help you?"

"Do, it's just be and da bears."

"What about bears, I don't understand?"

"The big won is trying to clib ub da tree."

"How old are you?"

"Dat doesn batter. I deed helb."

"Where are you? And don't say you're 'ub a tree'."

Eventually the bear cub went splashing into the water. The mama bear went splashing in after it. I missed lunch up the tree and almost dinner. I got down the tree late in the afternoon and found my way back in time to wash up and eat. My nephew and his two friends had volunteered for dinner service duties. The other chaperones complimented me on how such a nice young man he was.

Whatever.

The Modern Summer

There is a very nice young couple, well, not overly young, you understand, with a clever 8-year-old who live a few houses up the street from that good-for-nothing nephew of mine, who, if I thought I could get away with it, I would duct tape to the side of an intercontinental ballistic miss…and I would have good reasons, only I think I have wandered away from the starting point of this Ob-servation.

In it, my Ob-servation, I want to question whether today's busy summer schedule for children is the healthy, character-building regimen the medical community (body and mind) insists that it is. I can tell you straight out no amount of summer regimen of any kind did any favors for Oliver Ovid Ob. He's that good-for-nothing I earlier referred to. Do you know what he did one year in camp? He…again I am wandering. Sorry.

This poor 8-year-old (see above), in the summer I am remembering, was on a whirlwind tour of camp, park, library, ball diamond, cousins, court, pool, and bicycle path that would exhaust anyone who was older than nine. Kids are pretty resilient. But you had to think he hated it. This 8-year-old was a boy. His mother probably hated it, too. I think his father drank. In fact, I hope he did.

Mrs. 8-year-old drove their gas-guzzling van. If she didn't put fifty thousand miles on it that summer then I am lying to you. A bumper sticker read "…occer mo…". Obviously someone had tried to peel it off but didn't finish. Mrs. 8-year-old probably broke a nail or two in the process.

I saw the young boy a few times that summer. Every time but one it was as he was passing by in that van, sitting in the back, wearing a baseball cap, grasping a hockey stick, holding a basketball, clutching a backpack, adjusting helmet strings, gazing out the window, eating a pop tart, balancing a book on his head.

He seemed a nice enough lad when I met him late that summer coming out of the mini-mart near where we lived. "Hi," I said to him and he said back to me, "Hi, Mr. Ob." "How's your summer going?" I asked him. He stared at me for a moment, "Pretty good, I guess. My mom told me it's a great summer," he said. "She tells me that a lot," he added.

"Been busy?" I asked.

"Just regular, I suppose."

"Oh?"

"Yeah, you know, baseball, basketball, soccer, reading, camp, crafts, and some other things."

"Wow, that's a lot of stuff to do. Enjoying it?"

"Yeah, I guess so. My mom says it's fun."

"Your dad like it, too?"

"I don't know. He usually has a headache in the morning before he goes to work."

"Too bad."

"Do you know Ollie Ob?" he asked me. My ears perked.

"He's my nephew. You know him?"

"He lives on my street. What's wrong with him?"

Instead of launching into an expletive-littered answer that might wreck this kid's whole youth, I said, "What do you mean?"

"He tried to run me over with his bicycle the other day."

"I'm sorry to hear that," I said, containing my response so that this sweet youngster wouldn't get scarred by an angry outburst over my nephew's intolerable behavior. "Then what happened?" I asked him.

"I pushed him and he fell off his bike and scraped his knees and twisted his arm. He cried. I told him I was sorry."

I pulled out my wallet and handed the lad a $20 bill and three ones. It was all I had on me.

Conflict

Every successful dramatic story presents and resolves conflict as Miss Witherspoon told us when we were sophomores. We had no reason to call here a liar, but you know sophomores, which meant we called her, ahem, other names.

Back to this conflict business. In addition to finding it in great literature – Red Ridinghood and that wolf, the three pigs and that other wolf – we find it also in real life. Fortunately wolves and pigs usually don't play a role in real life. Conflict does. Now we're back to where we started. (How funny – a pork roast sounds very tempting right now.)

Moving on. The lobbyists for the leafy green caucus of the vegetable group have made serious claims of inadequacy towards the starchy constituency of tubers and their "inexcusable shortcomings as they relate to the furtherance of good health for human beings."

Do you see the conflict hanging in the air between these two? One can only gasp when imagining where the tomato might enter the fray if it weren't for its own conflicted existence, i.e., is it a fruit or a vegetable?

Miss Witherspoon, a bit of a tomato in her own right, did not try to help resolve this conflict of which I write. The fact of the matter is she left teaching before the veggie wars besmirched the landscape. Sophomores were heartbroken. Well, not the females. There is no gain in repeating any of the numerous rumors surrounding her departure and her subsequent whereabouts. Can we please have no more questions about Stella, er, Miss Witherspoon? This Ob-servation is on the topic of conflict.

And what larger conflict could there be than that between the forces of good and those of evil? (This Ob-server comes down foursquare on the side of good. Let there be no conjecture over that.)

You are reading this and you are speculating on just how that big brat of a nephew of mine will be introduced into the topic of conflict. You are well-aware of that kid's record and you know how disappointing he must be to his forbearing parents. He'd be Exhibit A in most studies where conflict is at the center, but not here and not now. Why? Because I tend to lose my temper and say (write also) things I wish to take back later.

Well, just one example. Perhaps you have seen that new restroom facility at the playground in the park over on Mountain View Ave. No? No matter. Certainly you saw the news coverage when it was discovered that the toilet seats had been super-glued closed. What? No? Gad, don't you pay attention to the goings-on around you? Never mind about that now. Just know that that bit of property damage had O.O.Ob fingerprints all over it, if you want my opinion. How he gets away with those things I'll never know.

We're coming to the end of this Ob-servation. We've been over a lot of instructional ground, haven't we? For example, leafy greens vs. starches. Which advances good health further? Have they been fully studied? Can they co-exist? I don't know.

That leads directly to the next question about conflict. And a real poser it is. Remember how deeply affected we were when we first experienced the trials of that Kansas girl and her weird companions? A scarecrow, a man made of metal and a two-legged lion? Their *pied de guerre* with witches and airborne monkeys and wizards? Conflict of the first order, don't you agree? The question I have is, did Dorothy Gale go through life thinking that whole ordeal was real? I'll bet she is on Facebook. I can ask her.

The point is that a toilet is of no use when its lid is super-glued closed.

Bully

When that disagreeable nephew of mine was younger, when we all thought his antics were "cute," or "adorable" or "where do you suppose he picked up that habit," he fell victim to a school bully. He would come home crying or moping or irascible. Only after several occurrences like this and our questioning did we learn about the bully. So his father went to the school principal to register his concerns.

I don't remember how it turned out exactly, but I do remember thinking about bullies and how they become one. I waffled over whether it might be a career choice. Then I thought maybe it's not a choice but just good basic training. The kid's old man may have been angst-ridden, who knows, or maybe he had unresolved issues with his "fellow man" leading to life lessons for the kid to steer him from victimhood to victimizer.

If there are published studies on the formative years of bullies, I haven't seen them. I'll put it to you that the accomplished bully gets his start around kindergarten. What better place? A classroom fitted with shy, frightened children.

"Anybody give you any crap today?" the old man quizzes his kid one day after school, probably in the first week.

"The teacher gave us name tags."

"Anybody stare at you?"

"Billy told me his dog died."

"Did you laugh at him?"

"He was crying."

"Good. He musta needed a punch in the eye. Give him one tomorrow."

"I don't have one."

"Sure you do. Here let me show you."

"Ow, that hurt."

"It's supposed to. It belongs to Billy. Give it to him tomorrow."

"I don't want to."

"Why, cuz you're a bellyacher?"

"I don't want to."

"And after you do give it to him, take his lunch away from him cuz I'm not making yours for school tomorrow."

"What for?"

"You want to eat, don't you? Sure you do."

After two months of assessments by the psychiatric staff and a protracted legal review by Board of Education attorneys, the parents of the burgeoning bully are invited in for a counseling meeting at which they first deny any aggressive behavior by their little boy then blame the teacher, the principal, the board members, the government, the PTA, the cafeteria and the other kids.

The school, its hands tied by decades of progressive disciplinary administration and a revolving door of academic ambiguities capped by state laws banning any authoritarian action potentially harmful to a student's "social development," agrees to continue to monitor the situation.

The old man laughs and tells his wife, "We skated on that one." The wife pours herself another drink. The kid, not yet in full bully bloom, has only a few friends. These he loses post haste, blaming "school."

Later when he picks on a new kid who gives as good as he gets, the bully kid complains to his old man. "Tell him," his old man instructs, "that your old man can lick his old man any day of the week. That'll show him." This the kid does.

The other old man, a cop and a member of the city's Swat Team, tells his son to tell the bully to tell his old man that Saturday works for him. He gave a time and named a place.

Wedding Day

It was a wedding day to remember. It was certainly a wedding day the main participants would not forget. They both said that. I heard them say it. In truth, everyone heard it. She was louder about it than he was. "I will never forget this!" is what she hollered.

But that came later. Later, too, than the attendees might have otherwise expected. You see, the ceremony did not get under way at the time listed on the pretty invitation. The officiant, who needed to be there as the state-licensed authority for marrying, failed to appear for a length of time. Once there he mumbled something about a sick car, a sick dog, and sick-and-tired of his wife, but he made little sense and no one was interested in excuses.

The organ music in the long interval got on people's nerves, not to mention the periodic phone ring. There was noticeable relief when we finally heard "The Wedding March." Gratitude as well for all of us who could see her as she stepped into view at the back of the church on her father's arm and as the scowl on her face turned into a smile. Left foot ahead, right step, left foot ahead, right step. She is lovely and smiling back and forth at her friends standing in admiration.

At this early moment her father detected that the seating arrangement was amiss. Upon reflection, some of us invitees concluded that it was an inadvisable time that he stopped the procession to ask the bride's friends who were sitting (standing at that particular moment) on the groom's side of the church to remove themselves across the aisle to the prescribed side. More than just asking. He directed us to get to the side where we belonged. The beautiful bride, his daughter, stood solemnly while two or three dozen people crossed the main aisle to comply.

An elderly man who evidently did not know who invited him began to cross the aisle but was turned back by a brash young usher who intervened to help the bride's father get things arranged according to tradition. Unfortunately, the elderly man was unaware that a photographer had repositioned his large tripod to steer clear of the migration. And, you guessed it, the elderly man collided with the tripod and sent it and the expensive looking camera onto the tile floor. The children present, who were having a great time running to and fro without a plan, thought the exploding camera episode was a highlight of the ceremony.

The officiant seemed unfazed by the disorder of the re-seating exercise. When it came his turn to conduct affairs, he began with discipline and warmth. "What did he say?" a woman asked. "Shh," she was told. "I didn't hear what he said," she said. "Shh," she was told again. She shh'd. Then the officiant spoke more. "What's he saying?" the obviously hearing-challenged woman said. "Be quiet, Irma," several people cautioned her. "Tell him to speak up," Irma said. "Shut up, Irma," someone yelled, quite impolitely.

The officiant interrupted his remarks and asked for forbearance. "What's that he said?" Irma asked. The offciant, now converted to conformity with the rest of the audience, said, "Can someone take Irma outside and get her a nice cup of tea so we can move along with this?" Someone led Irma out. "Where are you taking me?" she asked. "Who are you?" she added.

Toward the end of the rite and before the culminating "I do's" there was the "offering of peace and fellowship" which this particular congregation had been doing with its regulars for many years. At the appointed time, folks would turn to those nearby and shake hands or give a modest kiss or a friendly hug. In the name of peace and fellowship.

Unaccustomed to the unspoken territorial limitations dictated by crowded pews, three burly brothers rudely stepped over some guests into the main aisle and went some distance to where there was a stunningly attractive blonde woman who was doing some handshaking, some modest kissing and some friendly hugging.

The burly brothers arrived at her pew just as the "offering" was winding down. That did not deter them, nor did the fact that the statuesque woman (for she was) was in attendance with her husband. There were hurried and less than modest kisses and more than friendly hugs before the mister got his missus unclasped. It was a sticky situation. All the kids in church thought it was funny.

Despite the unconventionalities associated with the wedding, the two headliners agreed with their "I do's" to marry and we heard the offciant declare, "You may kiss the bride."

Pow! was the next sound. A car crash outside? No, because we also heard, "Mazel tov!" (It was not a Jewish wedding.) Someone had, in the Jewish tradition, stomped on a glass wrapped in a towel. "Mazel tov!" That was touching and thoughtful, if a little out of place.

That voice. That voice! "Mazel tov!" I recognized that voice. When I looked back down the aisle, there he stood with that dumb look he seemed to carry everywhere with him. My nephew. Oliver Ovid Ob. (He's not Jewish.)

He did not go over to the reception. You do not know the kind of trouble he might stir up. There were, however, three divorce lawyers in attendance all of whom were liberally passing out their business cards.

The Box

It was a good idea when it first landed on the table. It was a good idea during the planning process. It was a good idea when it was implemented. And it is still a good idea. Only thing is, not everybody got behind it with the same degree of enthusiasm as some others and with the proper spirit of cooperation.

Some while back I worked over a summer as a temporary employee in a vast stockroom of a large general goods retail chain. There was a large staff of full-time and permanent workers as well as some "temps" like me because the summer months were a busy period in advance of holiday shopping periods. The pay was okay.

I said it was a busy period and that is true. It meant we all had to be on our toes and be flexible. We all had times when we said something could be done better, and it was not just that we fire that do-nothing supervisor. Then it landed on the table. The good idea. Put up a suggestion box. You'll say "the deuce you say," but there it is. It was a good suggestion and it became real.

Before I go on with the "good idea" and how things turned out, I have to digress a moment. I took woodshop in high school and I was fairly handy around saws, planes, joiners and those things. So I said I would build the box. There were no other volunteers.

Thinking I would be doing him a favor, I enlisted my nephew in the fabrication project. We worked at it over a couple of weekends. When we were nearly finished with the box, my nephew asked me if he could put the last touches to it. Proud of his involvement, I agreed.

Some people just never learn and I must be one of them. With some fanfare, I attached the suggestion box to a pole in the stockroom at the end of work one day. The next day there was a hubbub around the box. When I went over, I found, like all my co-workers, that the suggestion slips were scattered all over the floor. Oliver Ovid Ob, my irrepressible nephew, had crafted the box in that last day of building fervor with a false bottom. What a harebrain.

I repaired the box at home with no help from any relations.

The plan was for our supervisor to retrieve the suggestions from the new box at the end of work every Friday. On the first Monday after that first Friday, our supervisor called us all together. He was red-faced. Was he ever.

For a do-nothing kind of guy otherwise, he sure did have a lot to say this day. He used words like displeased, hurt, outraged, betrayed. Of the three or four dozen suggestion slips in the box the previous week, he said, nearly all were very improper, particularly the personal ones about him and his wife.

I was directed to remove the box from the stockroom. So I got my tools and took it down. I went home thinking I could turn it into a mail box. Or a bird feeder. I determined, however, to do all the modification work on it without any "help" from O.O. Ob.

(John Thom writes:)
This is the end of Ob-servations involving that pus-ball nephew of Con Ob's. We now return to more of the "normal" Ob-servations.

The Ob-servations
Themselves, Even More Of

Looking Back

Lately I have been wondering if I don't exist in the back corners of someone else's imagination. I know that sounds, you know, crazy. I ask myself, do I "know" that or am I being manipulated by that other guy's imagination? When I say "I" is it actually him saying "you"? Makes one wonder…or is it him making me think I am wondering?

This all started one afternoon when I was watching television. Now normally I do not watch daytime television. Daytime television. Just those words scare me. They elude a definition that should entice rather than repel viewers. To think that daytime television advances day to day unabated in a land where we once accumulated such a strong majority of opinion that it could prohibit the manufacture, transportation and sale of alcoholic beverages baffles me. Yet daytime television persists.

That's how I feel, unless it is that other guy again pulling my strings as if I were a puppet. If it is that, if he is pulling my strings, he has managed to get us off the point. The point is the television. I was watching it when I began to get an overwhelming sensation. It didn't just whelm me, it overwhelmed me. I thought at the time, "Is that man watching me? The fellow on the television screen?"

Whoa! My first thoughts are hazy to me now, but an early one was, "Am I glad I'm wearing clothes." Worse was, "If I get up to go to the kitchen for another fudge brownie, will that television personality follow me there? And if he is capable of that can he follow me when the television set is turned off?" (An aside: It is the chronic self-deceiver who says he can carry a plate of brownies out to the front room to watch television and stop eating them whenever he likes. No, the answer is to leave them in the kitchen where you are obligated to get up and walk out to them one at a time with the goal of not overdoing it, as if you can overdo the eating of…oh, never mind.)

I'm just like the next guy who enjoys television shows and movies about paranormal themes and plots. I don't believe in that stuff, or I didn't until I had suspicions about that face on television that afternoon. I decided to test my theory. Wait, that's an overstatement. First, it was more a fear than a theory, second, maybe it was not "I" but that other guy's imagination again pushing my buttons. The test proceeded nevertheless.

What I did was, I stood up and tiptoed over to the wall near the front door to see if the face on television was still watching me. He was. Quietly, and unassumingly, I meandered across the room to an opposite wall. He was still watching me. To see just how clever the face was, I hurried into a back room to see if he was still keeping his eyes on me. All right, yes, okay, maybe that part of the test was ill-thought-out. I couldn't see him to see if he could see me. That still doesn't mean he wasn't watching me. I abandoned the test, but I held to my suspicions.

A few days later I was watching television in the afternoon, doing that surfing thing men like to do with the remote control. And wham! There it was. Just the situation I needed to suspect it again. What I discovered was that just about every other television program nowadays is a cooking show.

What better format for the television set to use to conduct its surveillance on viewers. It is the classic bait and switch. She shows you a sauce to pour over a chicken breast and you look at the sauce. You are thinking how delicious that herb chicken would be if it were on your dinner plate tonight. She is thinking how easy it is to eavesdrop on your house.

Is that bait and switch? Probably not, but the deed is done. What I want to know is why that cook is so interested in my front room.

Aesop Re-finished (I)

On one of my many trips into the dusty, dark and familiar palaces known as second hand bookstores, I once found a treasure of a book. It was a collection of the Aesop fables. What made it intriguing was something a previous owner had done. After many of the fables written by Aesop, this person added a short commentary or alternative ending suggesting a different interpretation from the original story.

I'd like to share some of these with you. In the interests of space and to skirt the laws of copyright, I have edited the original fable to a shorter version, though keeping the sense of the story intact so you will recognize it. Then I've added the ending penned in by the earlier owner word for word.

First, in this one, a fox wanted some grapes growing above his head along a trellis. Jumping failed him and he remained unfed as the grapes were just out of his reach. He gave up and spat out a useless rationalization. The writer added: "Stupid fox, why didn't you use a stepladder or stand on a box?"

In another, a milkmaid mentally conjured up a wealthy future based on selling her cream for butter. With the proceeds she will buy eggs for hatching into chickens and a promising poultry ranch. Then it's a gown she'll buy to lure potential suitors at a local fair. But she spills the cream and that means no butter, no eggs, no suitors, etc. Her dream is dashed. The mystery writer adds: "So she went to the fair and turned tricks and got real rich real fast."

Some dolphins and some whales had an argument that escalated into a real donnybrook. A sprat (whatever the heck that is!) interceded. But the dolphins and the whales, who wanted no help from a sprat, kept fighting. The writer added: "Greenpeace pulled up in one of its boats, took pictures and video of the whole affair and then sued the United States of America in federal court."

A walnut tree near a busy highway produced bumper crops every year but passersby mistreated it with sticks and stones to get the nuts. The tree, unhappy, said it was not cool that people did that to enjoy the walnuts. (That's it, the whole story.) The writer added: "If I were Aesop's creative writing teacher, this essay would get a D-minus. He is saved from an F only because he can spell."

A crow had a piece of cheese in its mouth. A fox wanted it so the fox complimented the bird no end, ending with a plea to hear the crow's voice. The obvious happened as the crow cawed and the cheese fell to the fox. The fox ate the cheese then hurled an insult about the crow's wits. The writer added: "Angry, the crow called upon dozens of his pals who perched above the fox and without letup delivered such a racket the fox went mad."

Jupiter and his new wife had a banquet and invited all the animals. They all attended save the tortoise which opted out. Jupiter later asked the tortoise why. The tortoise explained he was a home body. Perturbed, Jupiter ordained that the tortoise would forever be stuck in his shell so he'd always be a "home body." The writer added: "Soon a hail storm ensued and all of the other animals and gods were either killed or seriously injured. But not the tortoise safe in his shell."

A warren of rabbits, discouraged that they had so many enemies, resolved to end it all by plunging into a nearby pool. Whereat they noticed the frogs in the pond were afraid of them. Thus emboldened, the hares didn't commit suicide. The writer added: "Superior to the newly encountered amphibians, the rabbits quite accidentally discovered the delicacy of frog legs and made a small fortune selling the recipe to an itinerant Frenchman."

A dying farmer tells his indolent sons there is a buried treasure in the vineyard. "Go dig it up." They dig and dig but find no treasure even though the newly tilled soil helps to produce a bountiful crop. The writer added: "Meanwhile, their prodigal uncle, who incidentally owned a shovel of his own and knew where his brother was likely to hide things, was living *la dolce vita* at a faraway beach resort."

Aesop Re-finished (II)

There has been a loud clamor for more, therefore here are further adventures of Aesop, his menagerie of pathetic animals and the anonymous reader/writer who added his own comments to the fables I discovered in an old edition of the classics. Let's continue.

A wolf chanced upon a lamb. It was intent on a meal but was abashed for not having a reason to eat such a helpless foe. So he recites a litany of possible excuses, each countered cleverly by the lamb. Unrebuffed, the wolf leaps upon and devours the lamb. The writer added, "After a few burps, the wolf admitted it's nice to have a pleasant chat before dining."

A troop of thoughtless kids at the edge of a pool were throwing rocks at frogs, thinking it was funny, even killing some of them. Then a frog popped up begging the kids to stop. What may be amusing to you, the frog said to the kids, is killing us. The writer added, "Dibs, one of the youngsters shouted, aiming a rock at the outspoken frog."

A penurious old lady had two servants whom she worked hard. She had them rise each morning with the early call of the roosters. This displeased them so they caught the cock and wrung its neck. This did not deter the old lady who rose even earlier to awaken the servants. This also, presumably, displeased them. The writer added, "So they wrung her neck, stole her identity and cashed her social security checks."

A man had a lapdog and an ass. The ass lived in the stable, had enough to eat and did his chores. The lapdog lived luxuriously in the house, a favorite of the man. The ass became jealous and one day went into the house jumping around like the dog only to do quite a lot of damage. The man drove the ass unceremoniously back to the stable where the dumb animal remonstrated with himself for trying to be something different from what he actually was. The writer added, "The lapdog went out to the barn to console the ass, but instead he pissed on his leg."

This fisherman threw his net into the water and when he pulled it back he had only a small sprat. The sprat said he was only a small fish (oh, that's what a sprat is) and should be tossed back so he could grow big and be of use to the fisherman when caught again. The fisherman, unconvinced, said no because he probably wouldn't see the sprat again. The writer added, "Aesop got 50 cents a word for this tripe?"

A man went traveling and returned with exciting stories of his adventures abroad. In Rhodes, he said, he was in jumping contests and was unsurpassed. He added that you could go to Rhodes and people there would confirm his feats. Heck, if you are so good why don't you just prove it here, he was admonished. The writer added, "Thus was born the controversy, did Twain write Aesop?"

A boy swimming in a river got into trouble and almost drowned. His cries were heard by a man who told the boy he should not be so careless, but he did not help. The boy said you should help me first then scold me. The writer added, "The man said this way the lesson is more usefully learned, whereupon the boy swam to shore and told the man to eat shit and die."

A mouse and a frog became friends. Strange to say they tied themselves together to remain close. Anon, the frog went into a pool, the mouse drowned and the two were eaten as easy prey by a hawk. (Where does Aesop get this nonsense?) The writer added, "A hunter nearby shot the hawk, which was fly-ing slower than usual owing to such a heavy meal."

A boy got stabbed by a nettle while picking berries. He ran home cry-ing where he told his mother he barely touched the nettle. She countered by saying that it wouldn't have happened if he had grabbed it firmly. The writer added, "The boy grew up carrying this wisdom to become a politician. Ignoring accusations of nepotism, he appointed his mother to a succession of high-paying public office positions."

The Trouble With Aesop

The trouble with Aesop has been my mission for a very long time. Not the trouble with Aesop but my search for the trouble with Aesop. Well, it's not my search for Aesop's trouble, but rather the trouble with those fables he writes. Stay with me on this, will you? Aesop writes fables. I have come to the con-clusion that it is his writing of fables that is the trouble.

Whew. My mission is complete, except for sharing with you the wonderful insights of that mystery writer who inked such clever commentary after the fables in the book I discovered. Those Ob-servations are nearby. You just read them.

If I were Aesop my story would be over right at this point and that is the trouble with Aesop. His fables are so bloody short. Consider this, could you adapt an Aesop fable into a stage production? Or into a feature length motion picture? Anybody? Raise your hand if you know the answer. Here's a hint: no. I'll tell you why.

Don't hold me to this with precise precision, but if you look at Aesop and his fables, I think you won't find even one that begins with "Once upon a time," an opening that tantalizes you for the hour and a half you will spend with some exciting reading. Not Aesop. He goes right for the reader's throat. He'll say, "The dog was perched on the lily pad out of reach of his food dish." The Grimm brothers or that guy Andersen would spend pages and pages just getting us to that bowl of dog food.

Again, not Aesop and that's the trouble. Imagine you're in your favorite picture house to see an Aesop flick. You've bought your ticket. (Don't sneak in the way you did when you were a misspending youth.) You've got your popcorn, soda pop and a candy bar and you're just plopping down into your loge seat. The opening credits roll as the curtain parts. You set your soda on the floor between your feet as the music rises for the opening scene and you put the candy bar in your shirt pocket as the camera pans to a dog perched on a lily pad out of reach of his food dish.

You finger some hot, buttery popcorn as the appealing aroma tickles your palate. The dog barks once, a cat on a log floating past pushes the food dish a little closer to the dog, but still not near enough for the dog to reach it. Another mouthful of popcorn. A raccoon on another floating log does the same as the cat did. Another mouthful of popcorn and a sip of your soda. A tarantula emulates the cat and the raccoon. About one and one half minutes have elapsed as the screen goes dark and up pops: "Moral: You can never have enough friends."

There is no second feature and you go home wondering what the movie was all about. It cost you fourteen dollars for the ticket to the show plus another $12.75 for the popcorn, which you didn't finish, a soda, which got kicked over when people rushed for the exits, and candy bar, which melted in your pocket as you drove home. You feel grateful if you also did not have to pay for parking.

Grimm, Grimm, and Andersen, on the other hand, would have given you your money's worth. They would have milked that marooned dog for 80 or 85 minutes. Not only that but at the end you wouldn't have had to ask what it all meant. They would have spelled it out for you. The car chase, for example, would be a slick metaphor for the floating logs. At a conventional length for a movie, you would have finished your popcorn, wiped your hands clean of the tasty butter, sipped your cola to the bottom of the cup and languished through the candy bar with time to spare.

There's the trouble with Aesop.

A Wonderful Tradition

One year, because we went in a kind of rotation each Christmas Eve, it fell to me to recite the holiday favorite, "The Night Before Christmas." The grown-ups always enjoyed reliving the experience, one planned especially for the children who loved the story, which in their minds was coming true that very evening. All the young ones were sitting or lying on the floor near my feet. The grownups, nogs in hand, sat around the room, the fire aglow in the hearth.

"Twas the night before Christ..." I began.

"What?"

"I'm starting the story now. *Twas the ...*"

"What is that?"

"What is what?"

"What you said."

"It's the story, remember? It's 'The Night Before Christmas'."

"I'm thirsty."

"Okay, your mommy will take you into the kitchen for a drink. Ready now? *Twas the night...*"

"What's that?"

"What is what?"

"What's taws?"

"Taws? Oh, you mean 'twas.' That's just another way to say 'it was'."

"What was?"

"Twas means 'it was'. We call that a contraction."

"My daddy calls his car a contwaption."

"Does he? That's nice. Let's see, how about everybody sit real quiet while I read this fun story. You'll like it, I promise." Silence.

"Twas the night before Christmas and all through the..."

"Oww. Waaaaaa...Jimmy kicked me."

"I did not."

"Did so. Waaaaaa."

"Come with me," a parent said. "Waaaaaa."

"When all through the house not a creature was stirring, not even a mouse..."

"There's creatures in our house? What are they? Where? MOMMY!!!!"

"There are no creatures," I said, "settle down. It's just a story and the story says there are no creatures. Not even a mouse."

"I saw a mouse once."

"Me, too."

"Where did you see yours?"

"Kids, kids, kids, please, let's listen to our story. It's Christmas and it's a Christmas story." A couple of grownups got up to go to the kitchen, probably for more nog.

"The stockings were hung by the chimney with care, in hopes..."

"We have a chimbley."

"So do we."

"We do, too."

"All right, kids, that's nice. We all have chimbleys."

"Ha, ha, ha, ha, he said chimbley."

"In hopes that St. Nicholas soon would be..."

"Nicholas? Nicholas is in my school. Why is Nicholas in the story?"

"It's a different Nicholas, okay?"

"Does he pick his nose a lot?"

"What? Who?"

"Your Nicholas."

"I don't know. What difference does that make? Now be quiet and let me read this."

"I'm hungry."

"We just ate."

"I'm hungry." A parent took the hungry child to the kitchen. The two grownups were still in the kitchen drinking another nog.

"In hopes that St. Nicholas soon would be there."

"Where?"

"What?"

"Where is Nicholas going? You said he'd be there soon."

"Oh. Where? Here, I suppose. That's what St. Nick does."

"Who is St. Nick?"

"St. Nick is St. Nicholas. It's another name for Santa Claus."

"Santa Claus!! Santa Claus comes tonight!! Can we go see if Santa is here? Mommy, can we?"

"Let's hear the story first, hon."

"I wanna see if Santa is here."

"He's not here, hon. He comes tonight after you go to sleep."

"The children were nestled all snug..."

"Children were in nests? Why were children in nests? Are they being punished?"

"They were not in nests. Just listen to the story, will you, and be quiet."

"The children were nestled all snug in their beds, while visions of sugar plums danced in their..."

"What?"

"Oh, what now?"

"What's that?"

"What's what?"

"What you said."

"I'm reading the story to you. Can't you stop interrupting and just listen. You don't have to talk so much. Maybe some of your mommies and daddies could help out a little. Geez."

"Danced in their heads. And mama in her kerchief and I in my cap..."

"What's a kercheap?"

"Oh, for the love of Pete. Shut up! Don't ask any more questions, do you hear me?"

"Waaaaaaaaaa."

"Now look what you've done. And on Christmas Eve."

"It's not my fault. They wouldn't listen to me."

"They're just children."

"Brats, if you ask me."

"Now hold on."

"Okay, okay. Geez. Okay. Shall I continue or what?"

"Of course, we do this every year. It's a wonderful tradition."

"Right...okay...okay. *And mama in her kercheap, er, kerchief, and I in my cap, had just settled down for a long winter's nap. When out on the...*"

"Is Uncle Con going to take a nap? Why won't he read the story? I want to hear the story. Waaaaaaaaa."

"Hush, sweetie, he is reading the story."

"Not anymore I'm not. And you can stuff the wonderful tradition."

Oral Hygiene

The first signs of trouble can be very upsetting. A cold drink or an ice cream cone hits a tooth just right and clang! you are sent into orbit. It hurts. Brother, does it ever. Then comes the consternation of a trip to your dentist. Just what every fun-loving trooper desires.

You arrive and you are asked have you been here before. "Yes, I'm a regular patient." "Do you have insurance?" "Sure, just like always." "Your insurance card, please." "Here it is." "Fill out these forms and bring them back to me when you're finished." "Okay." "And no smoking." I don't smoke.

The delivery of health care keeps getting better and better you think to yourself as you are filling in the forms, the same ones you filled in six months ago on your last visit.

You hand the forms back. She says, "Okay, take a seat, we'll call you… wait…you didn't answer these questions." (You look.) "That's right, I'm not menstruating, I'm a man." "Oh, okay, sit down, we'll call you." (See, better and better.) You are called. It is your turn. You see the dentist.

"Having a little problem, are we?" he asks from behind his mask.

"Yes, it just happened. It hurt. I hope it's not serious."

"Oral hygiene is serious business, Mr. Ob."

"Oh, I agree. I was just hoping the problem is not serious."

"What kind of name is Ob anyway? Is it foreign?"

"It's just my name, I guess."

"Okay, open wide. Uh-huh, yup, I see, keep it open, please. You know what I think…nurse, hand me that number ten. Umm, huh, I see, yup. Okay, we'll need to look a little closer."

"Crowsher?"

"Yes, I see we'll have to do a little drilling."

"Drwillwing?"

"Yes, wide open, please."

"Awwww."

"Let's start with the posthole digger. The 12-inch blades."

"Okay, bud, but remember, we got until dark only and then we gotta close up."

"I know, whaddaya take me for?"

"Every six feet, too. Let's do those first. Then we can cut out all the crap we always find in there and fill it up with a sturdy redwood and some ready-to-set."

"I'll start cutting the posts."

"This one will call for a lot of wire. It'll look like a kid's retainer when we're done."

"We should tie it down with the rust-proof we bought last month."

"Good idea. We can see how it works on this opening."

"It'll be great, lemme tell you. It's like that thing when you say 'good fences make good neighbors'."

"That the only poem you ever heard of?"

"That's a poem?"

Oral Hygiene (II)

(Madrid Marriott writes:)

The Ob-servation we published yesterday, what can I say? I blew it. I am so sorry. Constantinople Ob had submitted two Ob-servations at the same time. While I was preparing them for posting, the first page of one got stuck to the first page of the other and the second page of the other became the second page of the first. I was eating a peanut butter and jelly sandwich at the time and some of the jelly dripped onto the pages. The first Ob-servation was on Oral Hygiene. The second was on building a fence. Again, I lost focus, I blew it and I am sorry. Onward and upward, I like to say.

Set In Your Ways

Don't get set in your ways. I got set in *my* ways one time and I recommend you don't get set in *your* ways. Here is why. Now listen because this is important. I wouldn't be telling you not to get set in your ways if it wasn't important or if there was any other way around it.

You see I've had bad luck buying shoes. Not just getting the right fit for comfort or the right design for healthy arch support, but also for appearance. Let alone cost. A big part of the problem, and it is a problem and don't try to talk me out of that, is the way you buy shoes. They look so inviting on the display case, all shiny and with the laces positioned so artistically in their little holes.

You tell the shoe clerk do you have this one in my size. He says what size are you. You say I'm not sure, about a nine and a half. He says...hold on. No, he doesn't say "hold on." I want *you* to hold on because the shoe clerk may be a woman in which case she is the one who would have said what size are you.

Well, there you are, another interruption in thought because I now have to explain that I am not pretending that shoe clerks are exclusively masculine in gender. I can't do these Ob-servations and constantly refer to third parties in both sexes. I can't say "he or she" at every reference. It just wastes time and space. And all these irritating interruptions. I'll bet that guy J.K. Rowling doesn't have to put up with this. He just types away and, well, I don't know what he does. It's not important anyway. Forget that.

Let's get back to the shoe store and the shoe clerk, can we?

So the clerk goes into the back and comes out with three boxes. Already you are starting to get nervous. Well, I am because this is about my bad luck in buying shoes, not yours. He says, for he was a man, he says, "I don't have your size in that style. I got these. They're close to your size."

I am in a shoe store. I am shopping for shoes. I have requested help. I have disclosed my shoe size. No one can mistake my purpose for being where I am at this very moment. Even though things are not going my way, I cannot just walk out of the store. So I sit down and take off my own shoes because he tells me to. He opens the first box revealing a shoe I would not wear to my nephew's wisdom teeth extractions (and you know how I feel about *that* kid.) Oh, and wisdom teeth? There's no way that jerk has anything close to resembling wisdom.

Back to shoes. The clerk fiddles with the laces, getting them into the holes just perfectly. He slips them onto my feet, tells me to walk around. "Stay on the carpet, mister, will ya? Look at them in the mirror, too," he says.

"Pretty nice, aren't they?" No, they are not, but I don't answer. Even though they fit just right, I tell him, "They pinch my toes, they're too tight." He tells me they'll stretch out with more wear. I am not convinced he has my best interests at heart. What else do you have I ask him.

Another box, more fiddling with laces, perfect through the holes, another trip around the store. "I told ya, mister, stay on the carpet, gosh." Uglier than the first, although fitting comfortably, these, I tell him, are too narrow and they hurt. Then take them off he tells me.

You'll recall that I warned you about getting set in your ways. Up front, at the start of this Ob-servation. Now here is where the rubber meets the road. A long time ago I got this idea about wearing cowboy boots. They looked so cool on the guys who wore them. I half promised myself that some day I would buy a pair. I was set in my way on this.

The third box opened to reveal a pair of cowboy boots. What spin of Fortune's wheel brought me, the clerk, this store, that day and that box into such a conjunction, I wondered. "Oh, he tells me, I didn't mean to grab this box." My heart skipped a beat. "Oh, I tell him, that's okay, let's take a look."

As there was no time wasted with fiddling with laces because cowboy boots do not have laces, I slipped into these quickly. Well, not so quickly. I had to find a smooth path for my toes and heels to get in without bending the boots sideways. (I told myself I would get the hang of that later on.) The neat pointy toes of the boots pressed my own toes together somewhat uncomfortably and the heels, 1-1/2-inch heels, by the way, cramped my own heels. It hurt. I recalled what the clerk said earlier about how wear would stretch shoes out.

I bought the boots. They were about three times more expensive than what I had planned to spend. A small treat for myself, I justified. I wore them out of the store. I was not more than 50 wobbly paces down the sidewalk when I stepped inadvisably on something on that 1-1/2-inch heel and turned my ankle about 45 degrees. The wrong way.

Everything after that is not instructive in the re-telling. Two things stick out, however. One, I have not worn those boots since that day. Two, remember what I said about getting set in your ways. You'll thank me.

The Comment

Standing there when it happened, I was not surprised by the comment. What was said was bull's- eye straight to the circumstance, although other folks in the small crowd missed, I think, the true target. The cast of characters in this little playlet included Mr. A, Mrs. A, young daughter A, and Sparky. Also Mr. B, Mrs. B, young son B, and Fido. Sparky and Fido are dogs. I don't know, just ordinary dogs. Their pedigrees are not relevant. No, I don't think they were purebreds. I wouldn't know how to tell anyway without asking. No, I did not ask. It didn't matter.

A man off to the side was watching the goings-on and it was he who uttered the comment. Before he did, the rest of the crowd saw the families A and B looking up into a tree line along the street where something had their attention. An animal of some sort was up there was the consensus. It was dusk. It was hard to make out what it was that was up there. And it was moving about a bit.

"That's the damnedest thing," someone announced. "Hey, watch your language," another criticized. "Aw, that's nothing," the first voice said. "Nevertheless," said the second. None of this exchange had anything to do with the comment that prompted this Ob-servation. It was, however, the damnedest thing.

The families A and B seemed bent on discovering just what it was that was up there. The parents were pointing and speculating. The young ones were jumping with excitement. The dogs were barking. This admission should not be taken lightly even though a barking dog is a redundancy. Dogs bark. A lot. And it's really hard to shut them up when they are on a scent.

Out came the comment. "You're barking up the wrong tree." How the man off to the side arrived at this conclusion with no evident evidence was surprising in itself. It was with the authority he delivered it that helped to divide the crowd into the camps about which the target of the remark was aimed.

The families A and B held fast to their interest above them, flapping their arms, pointing upward. The dogs had their front paws on the trunk of one of the trees yipping at what they thought might be something to attack and eat. Both dogs, not surprisingly, peed the tree.

Some in the crowd agreed with the man who spoke the comment that it was meant to mean the dogs were on the wrong tree. Others said no, it was meant to convey that the families A and B, and any others who had leant support, were on a fool's errand.

"What did you mean?" someone finally asked the man. There was no answer. "Come on, mister, you gotta tell us," another piped in. No answer. "All right, who said it? At least tell us that." No answer. It was dusk and the scene was getting darker making it harder to see who was where.

Either the man who made the comment had walked away or he was determined to not be found out. Come to think of it, another possibility is that he hadn't heard any of the pleas for his explanation over the loud dogs there. As I said a minute ago, I do not know which breeds these were, though one thing is for certain, and that is they were from stock with strong lungs.

Not About Busses

Except for the insidiousness of the accelerating encroachment of civil litigation when something goes wrong and an alert lawyer is around, the practice of shouting warnings of impending harm to others is still an honored tradition.

Who among us would not yell out, "Look out for that bus," if one were propelling in a traffic lane toward a pedestrian? It would come out more as a kneejerk, a split-second reaction to a perceived problem. Who among us?

Later, of course, you might also have a serious discussion with a pedestrian who would be so numb to his or her surroundings as to fail to see an oncoming bus. Busses in my part of the state are large. In yours, too, I am willing to argue. It wouldn't take a Hercule Poirot to collect enough clues to be able to announce that even a small bus should be enough to elicit a warning.

Don't get the idea that posting a printed warning on the front of that bus ("LOOK OUT!!") is going to do any good at all. Pedestrians, especially those numb to their surroundings, do not read busses, yet advertisers persist on buying the spaces on the sides of busses to call attention to their goods and services.

This Ob-servation is not about busses. It is about warnings. Warnings come in all sizes and shapes as the saying goes. They are also posted in numerous and obvious places: medicine jars; boxes of bullets; cigarette packs; wedding rings.

Those warnings, however, can be absorbed slowly and easily. You read how too many pills (or bullets) can be harmful to your health and well-being. You compare the maximum dosage to the prescribed number and you are on notice.

On notice. That's what this Ob-servation is about. To put another on notice when the other is in harm's way. Yet, and here's the thing, not everyone does it correctly. You can imagine, I'm sure, that an incorrect yell of warning could confound the yellee just enough so that he or she would miss the salient point of the yell.

A warning in widespread use is a good case in point. We all have heard it at one time or another or have seen it used in the movies either for dramatic effect or comedic relief. It is one commonly heard at construction sites. High rise construction projects to be specific.

"Look out below!"

Doesn't that warning conjure images of nasty consequence? Red hot rivets raining down. A heavy bucket of bolts kicked off a girder. An air conditioning unit loosed from a crane. Something as otherwise harmless as a lunch box. You calculate a falling object at thirty-two feet per second per second and you have a headache just waiting to happen. Even a hard hat is not protection enough to ward off these powerful objects.

A question then. Just who is the lummox who shouted the warning, "Look out below!"? That warning, from the lummox, is entirely misdirected. The answer to the question about who is the lummox is that he is someone who is not schooled in "the art of warnings." Had this construction worker attended class he would know how to alert people below of falling objects. For he would have correctly shouted, "Look out above!"

Consider. What's the first thing you're going to do when you hear in your vicinity, "Look out below!"? Yes, you are going to lower your head and look out below. In the meantime, this bucket of bolts is coming at you at thirty-two feet per second per second. That is considerably faster than the large bus we referenced earlier. Well, most busses. As you are looking around your feet ("below") for a reason to be on alert, you are also running out of precious time to be elsewhere when those red hot rivets reach your position. From "above."

The Art of Warning School. You just can't say enough good things about it.

Two, Please

A clever man once said, nay, a very clever man it was and he was saying that man, man in the general, universal sense, has not the five commonly agreed upon senses but rather he (remember, it's in the general, universal sense we're talking about here, so don't start that old argument with me again about "he or she") has seven senses. If you're nice and ask me later who it was who said this, I just may answer you, if you are nice and don't start any arguments.

The seven are sight, hearing, smell, taste, touch, sixth and humor. The first five combine to sum your surroundings. And so it was for me and Madrid Marriott on a fall Saturday when the air fairly crackled with crispness you could see, hear, smell, taste, touch.

Earlier Madrid had mentioned that there was a football game that very day at the college stadium. She said that would be fun to do. To go to the game. "Wanna go," she asked me, "it sounds like fun?" It did, so we decided to go.

Our senses were on high alert as we walked toward the football stadium. The leaves were multicolored, and having fallen on the pathway they crinkled under our steps; the pre-winter air was clean and hinting of the cold yet to come; the sky was filled with blue; mittens on our hands feeling of soft cotton were warming; and the growing crescendo of football fans readying for a competitive afternoon was music to our ears.

Up to the ticket window we strolled. "Two, please," I requested. "Two what?" "Two, please," I emphasized. I thought I'd said "please" the first time. "No, whaddya want two of?" "Two tickets to the game." It was a ticket window, for pity sake, what did he think I wanted two of?

"There ain't none," he responded. "No tickets?" "Yes, no tickets, the game's a sellout." Aha. "Now what do we do?" "That's up to you and the girl, fella."

There was a smarminess in his tone that was unmistakable, and I started to tell him I was not amused by it when he pulled a lever above the ticket window and closed the wooden door in my face.

Madrid was at my elbow through this whole conversation. She exclaimed, "No problem, we'll find a scalper." She said it with such matter-of-factness that I detected right away that she had done this before. "Come on," she told me.

The fall air fairly crackled with crispness one could see, hear…oops, I told you this already. But it was the case. "Him," Madrid said, nodding at a man standing alone fingering something. We walked over. "Hi," she said. "Hi," he said. "We hear today's game is a sellout." "Is it?" "Yup. Know where we can score two tickets?" "Two?" "Yeah, two." "It's a sellout." "I know it's a sellout, I just told you it was a sellout. What's that you got in your hands?" "These?" "Yes, those." "A couple of tickets." "Where are they?" "Twenty yard line. West side. Great seats." "Not bad," Madrid acknowledged. "Not bad? I'd say pretty good," the man said.

I was captivated by this give-and-take.

"How much?" Madrid said pointedly. "I paid twenty bucks each for them," the man said. "This is my friend Constantinople Ob," Madrid said, catching me way off guard, "and he'll give you forty bucks each for them." "Constantinople Ob? What kind of name is that anyway?" I hadn't said a word, but as the question was addressed to me I guessed I needed to answer it. "Oh, it's just my name." "Seventy-five each," the man continued. "Fifty," Madrid snapped, "and no more or I flash my badge and haul your ass in for scalping."

I gave him five twenties. "Not too bad," Madrid said as we walked toward the stadium gates, the fall air surrounding us like a cool blanket and more leaves crunching under our feet. Kickoff was time enough away to allow us to get in to our seats after loading up with hot dogs and chips and coffees.

At the turnstile, the ticket taker, a college-age fellow who looked as if he had been banned from football for being too big, took our tickets. I leaned forward full of anticipation for that special moment one always feels as he (okay, or she) walks through the tunnel that opens onto the field of play, the green expanse of grass, the contrasting school colors, the ceiling of blue sky, the gaily outfitted school bands, the chirpiness of the cheerleaders.

"Are you trying to be funny?" the big fellow said. Just prior to that question he had "placed" his rather large hand in the center of my chest, slowing – actually stopping – my progress toward that tunnel I just wrote about.

"Huh? What? What's the matter?"

"These tickets are for last week's game. You trying to be funny?"

I explained how we got the tickets, Madrid confirming my story. "You got screwed, mister. Now get out the way for these people who have tickets to *today's* game."

Dejected, I sulked away from the turnstile. "Let's go find that guy," Madrid said moodily, "and pound him." I could see she sensed that finding him was not likely.

On this day, my sixth sense – our sixth sense – had failed us. The seventh sense – humor – offered no consolation.

Confession

"Confession is good for the soul." Is it? Is it really? Many people like to say it is, believing there is truth in the oft-used statement. Let's see.

A man accused stands before the justice bar and explains, "Your honor, I confess that, yes, I did break into that jewelry store and take for my own possession diamonds, gems, gold, and trinkets galore, that I caused substantial property damage to the store, that I threatened sales clerks trying to attend to customers, threatened customers also, that I evaded arrest for quite a while speeding in a stolen car, putting innocent bystanders in mortal peril. I confess to these crimes."

The judge said, "That was one heck of a crime spree. The court applauds your new-found sense of right and wrong and is assured that your confession lifts a heavy burden, for confession is good for the soul, it is said. Nevertheless, I now direct the bailiff to slap you in irons and haul you away for many, many years. Confession may be good for the soul, but it stinks when it comes to the body."

"There is a time and a place for everything." Another oft-used statement which many people utter believing there is truth in it. Let's see.

A man who had been in a place of ill-repute arrived home in the small number a.m. hours. A woman, his long-suffering spouse, awaited him at the door. Later interrogation uncovered the fact that she was at first inclined to exclaim, "You are a slug." She, however, restrained herself assured that there is a time and a place for everything.

The man, more out of practice than regret, said, "Confession is good for the soul and I need to unburden mine for I have been concupiscent. I confess that I had too much to drink tonight at a facility popular with people who are easily led to questionable ends. My own behavior was inexcusable and through confession I hope to ease that burden upon my soul."

There is a time and a place for everything and it was at this time, when the man had finished confessing, and this place, just outside his front door, that the woman determined to express herself a second time. "You are a slug," she told the man. She also described a scenario in which the man, his soul unburdened, would learn through prolonged abstinence of a number of his favorite things that confession stinks for the body.

"Chickens will come home to roost." Not so oft-used as the other sayings we are ob-serving here, but there is a bit of truth in it, whatever it may mean. Let's see.

A man who held strong political convictions stood alone before a host of his party's influential movers and shakers and declared, "As confession is good for the soul, I need to tell you that I wantonly plundered the party's contribution coffers to my own personal gain. I removed hundreds of thousands of dollars and directed them to my own and others' accounts. I also solicited and received bribes to influence my votes. I unburden my soul in this confession and I feel atonement enveloping me."

At this time and at this place a man in the back of the room, joined quickly by many others, dashed out unholstering their phones. Reliable reports of the partially overheard conversations said this was to be the first disclosures of a rather widespread and messy scandal. Constituents of the many politicians, upon learning of the details of their wretched activities, were shocked, or so they said, recognizing how chickens do sometimes come home to roost, whatever that may mean.

To Buy A Hat

I went to buy a hat today because there is something about the out-of-doors that makes my face get all hot and red. I don't know what it is. Maybe the government should find out and take care of it. Only the hat industry, I suppose, will then raise a big fuss about lagging sales when the government solves the problem. I am not an advocate for the government to be the go-to guys to solve all our problems. But this is serious business. What's the government there for anyhow?

At the hat store the hat store salesperson declared, "Good afternoon." It was a friendly start. "How can I help you," he added all friendly like.

"I've been thinking about buying a hat," I admitted.

"Then what on earth are you doing in here?" His straight face discombobulated me and then made me chuckle as a twinkle brightened his eye. It was a joke. We were off on the right foot, for no one enjoys a joke more than I do. The odd thing is he was not wearing a hat. The clever merchandiser, I expect all the textbooks proclaim, features his or her products for the benefit of the prospective consumer.

"What kind?"

"Hmmm?"

"What kind of hat?"

"Oh. One that will keep my face from turning hot and red."

"A sun shade then." (That settled that. Hot, red, *sun*, hat, shade. Seemed to make sense.)

"Yes," I agreed.

"What style of hat did you have in mind? We have a wonderful variety."

"I don't know much about hats; I hadn't really thought about it."

"Allow me to show you a few."

(Time lapse.)

"Now, sir, what size do you wear?"

"Gosh, I don't know, 40 regular?" This made the hat salesperson laugh. I think he thought I was kidding. I wasn't. What hat sizes come in I could not tell you before today.

"Let's try one on, shall we," he said after he stopped snickering. "Ooh, that one's much too small. Here's another…ooh, still too small. Let me go in the back room and see what we have in our irregu…I mean in our big and tall selections."

As he stepped away I remembered that I am neither big nor tall. What the heck was going on, was I a character out of a Charles Schultz comics panel?

(Time lapse.)

"I am sorry we did not find a hat to fit you, sir. You know we will happily special order a hat from the manufacturer. My manager told me the hat company should be able to provide a hat to fit your, uh, dimensions."

I had to squint when I left the hat store into the sun – hatless and without sun shading – and I suspected everyone out there was staring at my dimensionally challenged head. This does not happen when I buy shoes. Nine and a half A. That's pretty regular.

Jabber

There I was once again called on to read a story, this time to a class of youngsters in an elementary school. "Choose something the children will enjoy, something colorful, with adventure and uplifting language," I was advised.

That suited me. I like adventure stories. Who doesn't? I'll tell you who doesn't, that dull nephew of mine. I once tried to persuade him to read *Treasure Island*, the rollicking-good tale by Robert Louis Stevenson, a favorite of any lad I have ever known, except for that unrequited lazybones. He said… well, what he said is not pertinent now. It was another opportunity, however, to wash his mouth with soap.

Back to the reading at the elementary school. They were third graders. The reading hour was just after their lunch period. Those who had no desserts in their lunches lay their heads across their arms on the desktop either fighting to stay awake or giving in to sleep. Those with sugar treats were on the verge of open rebellion.

"Class, this is Mr. Ob," the third grade teacher revealed. I smiled. "What's a misterob?" one of the sugar-laden students asked. "Why, that's his name, Richard," she answered. "It is? What kind of a funny name is that?" Richard pressed. The teacher looked at me. It seemed she wanted me to address the question. "Oh," I said, "it's just my name." Richard rolled up a piece of paper and threw it at another student. "Richard!!" the teacher admonished. "What?" Richard said by way of a defense. "Children, pay attention, please. Mr. Ob will read us a nice story."

"Pardon, but it's not exactly a story," I corrected. "It's a poem. There's a story in there, but it's really a poem." "Whatever," the teacher replied under her breath, though I did hear her.

I started. "The name of the poem is 'Jabberwocky'," I told them. There was some stifled laughter. The teacher seemed to raise her eyebrow. "It's great, a famous well-known poem by Lewis Carroll. You know who Lewis Carroll is," I told them, "he wrote *Alice In Wonderland*." "That's a cartoon," one of the students called out. "Yes, that's right," I agreed, "but it started out as a book before it was made into a cartoon."

"Read *Alice In Wonderland* to us," another student weighed in. "No," I answered, "it's much too long and we would not have enough time to finish it. This poem will be fun. I am sure you will like it. It's different."

As I wiped my reading glasses and placed the sheet of the poem on the desk in front of me and glanced at the teacher and prepared to start the poem, I felt a calmness. I was calm, the teacher was calm, the room was calming. I closed my eyes for a moment to harness my breathing and then opened them and began to read.

"Twas brillig and the slithy toves..."

I love the poem, its rich imagination, its inventiveness, its simple story locked in a compelling rhetoric. I read on as though I was all alone in the classroom "...*Beware the Jubjub bird...took his vorpal sword in hand...through the tulgey wood...went snicker-snack...my beamish boy...and the mome raths outgrabe.*"

Without looking up I let my eyelids roll closed and I let my mind envision Carroll's field of combat where the Jabberwock was beheaded. I hoped the children in the class that day could also experience the panoply of the poem's exultant expression in their own minds' eyes. It was gratifyingly quiet.

The little buggers. It was quiet because they were all asleep. Did they hear even one word I read? I turned to query the teacher whose own head was drooped to her shoulder. I was thinking about slamming the door when I left the room.

Bermuda

It just lurks there, acting all innocent, bringing no unnecessary attention to itself, distracting us, actually, with that triangle "myth," thinking we would not eventually wake up to the potential threat. What's a mere 667 nautical miles today with the array of military and technological advances available on markets – regular and black – for anyone to turn into an adversary? Go look at a map. A globe is better because it offers a sobering perspective.

It just lurks there. I said it is 667 nautical miles. That's from North Carolina! In the good old U.S. of A! A safe distance? Convert that to real miles – American miles – and it's a mere 580. A lot closer than you thought, am I right? Innocent? The Ob camp wonders. Let's examine the record.

Bermuda is a U.K. possession. I looked it up. U.K. is the United Kingdom. Know who is in the "United Kingdom"? England. Yes, the same England who used to own us. Sellers remorse? There's something to that, don't you forget. We bloodied their nose back in 1776 or so and they crawled away with their tail between their legs. Or did they? Have you noticed that they slithered north? Uh-huh, Canada. A lot closer than Bermuda. Are you following this?

It's a red herring, people. Canada is. All friendly and neighborly? No, a U.K. pawn is what Canada is. Sitting there offering no animosities, patting us on the back when we do good deeds, and all the while drawing attention away from, yes, Bermuda. I don't like the smell of this whole geographical coincidence either, if coincidence is what you believe in.

The claims Bermuda tries to make as if we are going to buy into their sun-showered, short-panted conviviality because there are but 20 square miles to the place. Twenty? How many offshore banks are based there swimming in money, money anyone could use for nefarious schemes. When will people wise up? Troy, Byzantium, Holy Roman, how big were those behemoths when they pushed other empires around? Probably more than 20.

The capital of Bermuda? Hamilton. Talk about your clever deceptions. The same name as that of our martyred Alexander Hamilton in a duel in 1804 by the dastardly Aaron Burr. Do you want to guess where Burr's ancestors were from? Well knock me over with a Tower of London raven's feather…it was England.

Do I even have to remind you of 1812? The War of 1812? With England? Come on. How the cowardly Englanders impressed – stole – the innocent, God-fearing American sailors who plied the oceans with goods "Made in America"? And who, in 1814, burned the White House to the ground? Do I have to spell it out to you?

Now put this on your plate and try to swallow it. It's 1995 and a U.S. naval air station is closed. Closed in Bermuda. Did you, like me, have assurances that at the time England was our ally? 1995 is not so long ago. It's still 1995 and what do voters do in Bermuda in a referendum aimed at independence from England? They reject it overwhelmingly. Do you wonder just how many hanging chads helped to cloud that outcome? Who gained from that vote? (Uh, England is the answer, you don't have to look it up.)

Heard enough? No, I didn't think so. And that brings us back to the triangle, a place where unexplained disappearances into thin air of airplanes and ships have occurred for a long time. Here's the kicker. Draw a triangle in that notorious part of the Atlantic Ocean and you have North Carolina at one point, Florida at another. The apex of the triangle? Are you sitting down? Bermuda! The Bermuda Triangle!

P.S. You have just finished this Ob-servation and you may think something in it is amiss. I have to apologize. When I was explaining the threat, I managed to mess up the separation between Bermuda and the U.S. when I calculated the nautical miles and the statute miles. (As I have told you before, mathematics is not my long suit.) The distance is 580 regular miles and 506 (not 667) statute miles, which, if you are of a like mind with me, is evidence that the threat is edging closer. As the clock ticks and the ocean shrinks, do you ask, as I do, who is on watch in this crisis.?

P.P.S. Now wait just a minute before you climate change activists jump down my throat because of the reference to "ocean shrinks." Constantinople Ob is locked elbow to elbow in the front rank with those who are in desperate grief over how our beaches – what else beyond that? – may disappear in decades ahead as Earth warms and melts its ice reserves up north. The reference to "ocean shrinks" has only to do with the frightening proximity of Bermuda to our East Coast citizenry revealed in this Ob-servation where the menace is the equal to rising tides.

Smell Fear

"They can smell fear, you know." Oh, and here's another one, "Only the female bites." Let's get real. What have we learned? What lessons do we take away?

Start with that first one ("They can smell fear"). Who is "they" is a good place to begin. If memory serves, "they" is an animal, a not-so-timid animal, and not one of those nocturnal ones who eat and play at night because they are pretty high up on the prey menu. "They" is almost assuredly going to be an animal with some "hair," one that has size, one with teeth and claws, one with a nose for fear. Been there, it says, done that. If you are confronted by one of these animals, well, good luck.

The moral of this Ob-servation, if we did morals, would have been to advise (1) stay the heck out of jungle clearings, and (2) if you had to be there, be sure to wear your "I AM FULL OF FEAR, YES" sign prominently across your chest. There is no good reason to give that animal time to sniff out your fear status. Just point to your sign, wave goodbye and disappear into the dark.

What does fear smell like, you ask. Probably a combination of denim, aftershave and beer.

Now to that other one ("Only the female bites"). In this case I am pretty sure that we are talking about smallish, airborne insects. The mosquito comes to mind. Damnable creatures with absolutely no apparent redeeming characteristics. In their shockingly short lifespan they sleep all day rising about ten seconds past sunset, land on your arm or ear or ankle and put a bite on you that'll leave a welt the size of a nickel. "Job well done," her mate congratulates her when she gets home.

She. "Only the female bites." If that's true, what's he do all night? Out with the boys playing poker? Back to her for a minute. The presumption here is that she speared you with that long honker of hers to suck blood from you to nourish herself. If that's true, and "only the female bites," where does her mister go to get dinner? Doesn't make any sense. He's gotta eat, too. We doubt seriously that him and his pals are knocking down baloney sandwiches and potato chips at that poker party. Doesn't make any sense.

Next time one of those interlopers lands on your arm and ties a napkin around its neck ready for dinner, grab her (or his) ass and go and get the microscope from your chemistry set and make an examination to determine its gender. Three will get you five you find a man among the swarm. Otherwise, doesn't make any sense.

Nothing New Under The Sun

Some people like to say there is nothing new under the sun, and your humble servant (that's me) is apt to agree. So it happened that during the locally infamous dust-up between the Webilditfast Construction giant and the Webilditcheap Development Co. a difference of opinion arose over a shipment of building materials. What else when the contentiousness is between the above-named private companies? It certainly would not be over the…oh, never mind; let's move on, you are distracting me and everyone else with your look of disbelief.

The difference of opinion led to a letter containing unfortunate language countered by another letter suggesting in retort that the other company's executives had dubious parental histories only to be followed by retained lawyers exchanging stern challenges and consequent arbitration hearings where coarse hand gestures led to finger pointing which got close enough to be called a poke that did not go unanswered in the way of a push that came to shove and you know where that always takes you. The hearing arbitrator got a black eye out of the deal and he doesn't even work in construction.

"Golly," he said.

He was quoting the best paragraph in Evelyn Waugh's "classic" novel, *Brideshead Revisited*, a molasses-paced traipse of Oxford effetes through the uneventful drudgery of 1920s and 1930s England peopled by characters with the least appealing charm in the universe and propelled with unexcelled prolixity to a pointless abyss. It was Waugh's "masterpiece" said one reviewer. "Golly, he said," says it all.

More trouble ensued between the construction companies.

The police admitted there was insufficient evidence to lead to arrests over the complete collapse of the under-construction office building on Grand Avenue. What a mess. "It took a real pro to undo the supporting engineering of this building," an investigator claimed. "But who?" he had to ask. The debris was owned by the Webilditfast guys. The Webilditcheap crowd said they were "out of town" that Saturday night. Actually, some of them were. An alibi.

A week later the sheriff admitted there was insufficient evidence, so no arrests following the fully laden runaway cement truck that plowed lickety-split along a path through a block-long, half-built strip mall in county territory a mile or so east of Grand Avenue. The resulting pile of junk was owned by the Webilditcheap guys. The other crowd had filed a stolen truck report with the sheriff about thirty minutes before the "unfortunate event." An alibi.

Then events turned nasty.

What happened was the "nothing-new-under-the-sun" thing. For weeks construction in this area was slowed by workers pre-occupied with a zone defense. If a site went unattended it unaccountably got vandalized. Hmmm. So electricians and carpenters and plumbers and day laborers found themselves patrolling construction perimeters.

Webilditcheap had a contract to build a self-storage warehouse just west of Bill Clinton Avenue, and, like so many other projects, progress was real slow. With one eye on a joist and one eye on the lookout for Webilditfast thugs, joists didn't get hung quite so fast as in more peaceful times. (I know it's a dangling participle or something. Get over it. Just read on. It's the story that counts.) When the situation got so bad that it affected company profitability, decision makers made decisions. At Webilditfast, the bosses said enough was enough. They said it to Webilditcheap workers at the self-storage site.

A cease fire.

Nothing new under the sun, right? As a show of good faith Webilditfast offered Webilditcheap a going away gift. Webilditfast would be going away but leaving the gift. The gift was a delivery truck loaded with about a dozen portable toilets, the kind you see all around construction areas, the kind that meet a real need in that industry. The truck was delivered and parked just outside the main gate to the construction site.

After the Webilditfast guys left for wherever they needed to go, the Webilditcheap guys drove the truckload of potties into the construction yard and went back to their duties. Evidently no one who worked for Webilditcheap had read the *Iliad* and could recall the reference to the Trojan Horse. If so, they would have caught wind of the "nothing-new-under-the-sun" refrain, because that night Webilditfast guys, who had been hiding in the potties, sneaked out and overpowered the remaining Webilditcheap guys. Don't you see? The "Trojan Shitter" was established as a modern tactical brainstorm.

Tap Shoes

A cat and a mouse walk into a tavern. They are wearing tap shoes. Click, click, click, click all the way to the bar. The cat jumps up onto a barstool. The mouse, smaller, cannot leap like a cat and cannot climb up the legs of the barstool mostly because of the slippery taps on his tap shoes. "Squeak," he says, uttering a mouthful. "Meow," the cat replies, explaining his plan. The cat jumps to the floor where he lies down to allow the mouse to crawl onto his back. "Meow," says the cat turning his head toward the mouse. "Squeak," says the mouse before securing his grip in the cat's fur.

How the cat, with the mouse hanging on, jumps up onto a barstool, allowing the mouse to alight onto the stool's seat, and how the cat nimbly jumps onto the next barstool does not need description here. Suffice to say it happened.

"I don't know where to begin," the barman says to his new customers. "I have lived a long time and I have traveled to mysterious places and I have been in the army and I have experimented with hallucinogens and I have been expelled from parochial school. I have seen it all, or so I thought. You may not believe what I am about to tell you – in support of my comment about having thought I had seen it all – but I once served as barmaster where a mermaid and a unicorn came in. It is true. There is a record of it."

(At closing time that night the barman confessed that his period in youth when he experimented with hallucinogens was foolhardy. He said he has since taken opportunities to counsel youngsters to foreswear drugs. "A wiser way of life" is how he called it.)

"Yet you two…" The barman stopped and surveyed the tavern. "Anyone have any questions for our new friends here? I just don't know where to begin." Equally dumbstruck by the oddity of a cat and a mouse wearing tap shoes and sitting at the bar of a tavern, no one spoke right away.

Then…"Ask them what'll they have," a discerning patron said. Someone else laughed. The barman looked back at the cat and mouse. "I have lived a long time and I have traveled to, etcetera, etcetera," he said, waving his hands, "and it takes that fellow over there to remind me that I have training in my profession and years of experience back upon which I should fall and perform my duties. Therefore, what'll ya have?"

(Also at closing time, after the barman had lightened the burden on his chest about his partially misspent youth, he said his expulsion from parochial school was not for any faults of his. "I got blamed for everything after that one time I locked the girls in their restroom. Okay, two times.")

The cat turned to the mouse. "Meow?" The mouse thought for a moment. "Squeak," he answered. The cat said, "He'll have a Bloody Mary and I'll have a dry sherry. I feel festive." The barman, trained and experienced in mixology, fashioned the drinks and put them on the bar top. "Thanks," the cat said, "it would help if we had straws. No thumbs." Straws arrived.

The oddity of the situation in the tavern was unchanged, but the barman and some of the patrons were growing more accustomed to it. "You can talk," the barman observed. "And we're bilingual," the mouse said, using English for the first time. "Bilingual?" "Sure," the mouse offered. "He speaks feline and English and I speak rodent and English."

(The time in the army, the barman revealed at closing time that same night, did not include any hostile action. "I was in the Quartermaster Corps. I issued a lot of fatigues and mess kits. I really couldn't carry that experience back into civilian life.")

"Bilingual," the barman said. "A cat and a mouse. Think of it. But wait. When you talked earlier all we heard were 'meow' and 'squeak' spoken. That's not English. It's onomatopoeia. That's not a language. How do you understand each other when one speaks feline and one speaks rodent?"

"What'd I say, bilingual?" the mouse answered. "I meant trilingual."

"That makes more sense."

"Could we have another round, please," the cat intervened after some time had passed.

"Of course," the barman complied.

Drinks served, the barman was about to speak again when the cat said, "You haven't asked us why we are wearing tap shoes."

The barman asked.

"We're vaudevillians. We're a song and dance act. In these tough economic times and with the MTV demographic dominating taste, and talent agents reluctant to hitch their wagons to these stars (here he pointed at himself and the mouse) we have to be ready to perform anywhere anytime. We're not street performers; don't call us that. We just need to be flexible."

The barman wiped the bar top.

"Do you book acts in this tavern?" the mouse asked.

"No," came the answer.

"Well, what's the tab?" the cat asked.

"Two Bloody Marys, two sherrys, twenty-six dollars."

"As you can see," the cat offered, "we do not wear clothes, so we do not have pockets. We are not sporting fanny packs or brief cases where we could secure a wallet. Bottom line, we have no money."

"You have no money."

"We have no money."

"How did you propose to pay for drinks in a tavern where they are not served for free?"

"We made no proposal or provision."

"That seems odd to me."

"That's odd? Me and a mouse walk in here in tap shoes, converse with you and down your drinks and you think it's odd only that we have no money?"

"Yes, odd."

"I find *that* odd," the cat said.

"What you find odd don't mean squat to me. Out back I have a German Shepherd. He's hungry and he's upset because he has not been fed. Under the bar here I have a double-barreled shotgun. Under the shotgun," the barman said turning to the mouse, "I also have a mousetrap. It's true we do not book acts in this bar, but that doesn't mean we do not do improv theater."

"Gulp," said the mouse.

"Oooo," said the cat.

"Somebody," shouted the barman, "go get Adolf. Put on the protective covering before you let him off his leash."

When To Paint Your Dog

During the daily staring contest I had with my dog this morning, it occurred to me that he hasn't been painted in a couple of years. Just more fallout from the distracting events bombarding me – and you, too, I'll bet – from the electronic gadgetry swarming around us fourteen hundred and forty minutes a day. It seems I can't get a thought in even edgewise to keep pace with my own responsibilities and simple desires.

But this is not about the oppressive conventional and social media phenomenon. I'll be surprised if you tell me you do not know how I feel about that. I am sure you know how to read between the lines in my Ob-servations.

No, this is about painting dogs. Until today, I went around believing that loads of people painted their dogs before I stopped into a pet shop new to my neighborhood. Not "What color?" or "How thick is his coat?" nor "Brushes or spray cans?" No, it was, "What are you thinking!" Not a question, more like an accusation. When I made my plea – "It's only a dog, not a cat" – the saleslady expressed herself in most unladylike terms.

So I went to a paint store. Let me remind you of what I wrote just moments ago. I am easily distracted by the bull-rush of electronic oratory in my life which explains why I did not think "paint store" before I thought "pet shop" when I wanted to equip myself for the job of painting my dog. I won't make that mistake again.

The salesman at the paint store interrogated me carefully in the way professional service people do when they have been trained well and aim to promote customer satisfaction. His first question washed away any angst I may have been carrying after exiting that new pet store. He asked, "How long since you last painted your dog?" Ah-ha, an understanding young man. When I told him it was about two years, I could see his face fall just a small bit betraying his disappointment in me. He recovered quickly, then he tactfully and thoughtfully counseled me on some of the disadvantages at going more than nine or ten months between dog paintings. I listened attentively because he is in the paint business and I am not.

The purchases to get the job done right came to more than I had expected to pay, but again, the young salesman is the pro, not I.

At my car in the parking lot as I opened the trunk lid to put in the paint and other painting materials, two fellows – college age, I assumed – passing by saw my dog in the trunk and one gasped, "What kind of dog is that?" Before I had time to answer, the other fellow said, equally surprised, "Never seen a dog that color before." The second comment, the one about never seeing that color on a dog before, triggered my immediate response which was, "You are not likely to see it again because I am going home to re-paint him. I have chosen a new color."

Guido, my dog's name is Guido, looked up at me from the floor of the trunk. I sensed the tension in his demeanor. I sensed that he was challenging me to another staring contest after he had lost three days in a row. It would have been four days in a row, only he is not allowed to answer the telephone when it rings. I am.

Brainpower

It is known that the human being has a brain with the same size and mass as a large baking potato. It is not known how many human beings have the brainpower of a large baking potato. Studies have mixed findings to point to a helpful answer. There are tests in schools; they are inconclusive, except at the pubescent high school level. There are periodic local, state and national elections; they are conclusive, showing little or no brainpower in either the elected or the electorate. There are movie stars who speak on public issues without the benefit of an approved script; they are very conclusive, revealing that their brains are truant. There are athletes who speak when off the court or the field or the diamond; they are really, really conclusive, revealing that their brains are in a small jar in the team doctor's locker.

Study managers are still looking for human beings to test where the findings will be more encouraging. In the meantime, farmers in Idaho are boosting production of the state's iconic crop with the expectation that there will be a rush by the scientific community for volunteer subjects to have their heads examined for the purpose of a possible transplant. A potato for a brain.

Farmers in Mississippi make the counterclaim that their state's famous product is the one that should be utilized in any transplant program. A spokesperson said, "A head stuffed with cotton will be as thought-promoting as a potato, and we have many examples in universities across the country where that's true."

Ranchers in Texas are up in arms over the debate that fails to include a by-product in volumes ample enough to satisfy even a seemingly insurmountable demand. One rancher, and I issue a warning here of some indelicate language to come, makes the argument that "there's loads of folks here and about and in other states who have shit for brains and appear to get along just fine. Hell, I vote for them every time. Long as they are Democrats acourse."

An undertaker in Chicago, while expressly denying that contraband body part trafficking occurs in Illinois, said, "There ought to be a law that allows my profession to, how can I put this, to, uh, to recycle the brains of our client base. We would have the means to properly fit one brain from here to another cranium there. They're there for the taking. I mean, you know, in the legal sense. They're dead anyway, so what's the big deal?"

The National Association of Rock Quarriers, when advised of the farming output up in Idaho, issued a statement reading in part, "Based on our honored history and a concentrated campaign to rub out the malicious innuendo of 'rocks in the head," our members stand unanimously in opposition to any efforts to study our product as a substitute for the human brain. The IQ of just about any rock is materially higher than the average voting-age Californian, for example. The gap only widens as the human being ages. We're not going to dumb down our rocks just because studies tell the truth about you people."

When the issue was at a fever pitch, one of the cable news network prime time programs sent a reporter to Walter Reed Army Medical Center in Washington, D.C. It is the home of some of the most advanced diagnostic and treatment regimens in America. The reporter's assignment was to get an up-close-and-personal look at the progress being made. Brushing the blond hair from across her well-shadowed eyes and brimming with a drop-dead-gorgeous smile, the reporter spoke into the camera, "Am I on or what? Tell me when I'm on. Oh, I am? Good. Good evening, I am standing here in Rochester, Minnesota, just outside the doors of the Mayo Clinic...what? Where? Well, why didn't somebody tell me?" I cite this as not really a test, but as an example of the relative potency between potatoes and brains.

H And G

Okay, I'll come clean. Yes, what I did was regrettable. What I did was read the fairy tale "Hansel and Gretel" to a few of my young nieces and nephews. No, not that boob, Oliver Ovid Ob, the nephew I've told you about before. He wouldn't listen to a story if it were a roadmap to a lottery prize. The way he doesn't take interest in anything you'd think he was as dumb as a stump. You wonder what they do in the schools. Ah, yes, I've figured out how he manages to "pass." The teachers just don't want him back for another year in their classrooms.

My other nieces and nephews had the courtesy to listen as I began the classic fairy tale. For my part, I had not read "Hansel and Gretel" in many years so the experience was going to be a heartfelt trip back to my own youth.

The little tykes were wide-eyed before I finished the first paragraph. You remember, it's the one that mentions that H and G have a stepmother (universally a nasty character in children's literature, I'd say) who does not love the two kids. Next my kin learn that the stepmother has talked H and G's father into abandoning them in a forest. They're crying now, my nieces and nephews. The story does not reveal if H and G cried.

I persist. Hansel has a clever plan to find their way home. They make it. The crying has reverted to just a sob or two as the kids recognize there is hope. Whereupon that trip into the forest is not only agreed on again by the father at the stepmother's insistence, but also Mr. Dad takes the kids even deeper into the woods. This time Hansel's escape is trumped by some birds and the kids are crying once more and are very sad.

This is a "fairy tale."

The crying turns to hysteria when the kids learn that Hansel and Gretel are grabbed by, big surprise here, a witch. A witch who plans to fatten Hansel so she can eat him. A couple of the kids are prostrated on the floor almost comatose.

I again persist. I can't stop. It's an irresistible force. What in heaven's name is going to happen next? How can I stomp all over the youthful innocence of these relatives of mine? It happens that it becomes Gretel's turn to display some cleverness. This she does by pushing the witch into a large oven and slamming the door shut with a consequence the author does not enlarge upon knowing we get the idea.

I quickly go on to the part when H and G discover a treasure trove at the witch's cottage (it's in the story, honest) and take it home to daddy whose harpy of a wife is no longer there. Happiness reigns.

I am not invited back to that house for many months, I don't get birthday cards from them that year, the annual summer family reunion barbeque is held without me, and somebody toilet papers my magnolia tree. That last thing I lay at the feet of O.O. Ob. Sounds just like him.

Six Bits

The barber was an anachronism. A thirty-ish man, if you can believe that. By simple observing, I argue, barbers – or hair stylists as so many are known now – are women mostly. The tonsorial profession, an honorable one for sure, was male dominated until around mid-March 1994 when female practitioners came on the scene in big numbers. Something in the water?

A row of barber chairs staffed by a squad of barbers (what else?) and you have the makings for a rousing good time. This shop, by the way, is the one with an all-male crew, including that fellow I mentioned above. I can't tell you his name. I didn't ask him. He didn't offer it either. This is a barbershop, not a Moose Lodge. People don't walk in and introduce themselves to the proprietors. Just not done.

All the chairs were occupied by customers. The guy giving a cut at the end of the row says to his customer, "Heard any good jokes lately?" The guy getting the cut says, "No." Only "no." Not "no, what about you?" Only "no." Even with the snip-snipping and a little buzz-buzzing from the other chairs a silence clung to the air.

Moments passed. Don't know how many, no one was counting. Doesn't matter anyway. More important was the silence. It was stifling. Some might say it was an awkward moment. To cut into the tension, another customer volunteered, "Hey, stop me if you've heard this one." What a relief. Now for some jollity to relieve the sour mood. Except… "Stop." That from the guy getting the cut at the end of the row who earlier announced "no."

"You have got to be kidding, I didn't even start the joke, so how do you know if you have heard it?"

"Heard 'em all."

- "You've heard every joke?"

"Yup."

"That's impossible."

"Why?"

"Why? Why's it impossible? Because there's millions of jokes, mister."

"Heard 'em all."

Again silence hung in the air. Surrounding the silence was the same tension that the other customer hoped to cut. An edge of sullenness could be felt. Snip-snip, buzz-buzz. This was not a happy barbershop. This was not a place for jollity that day.

The bell above the door shouted its tinkle-tinkle shocking all of us out of our disbelief. ("Heard 'em all.") A man in need of a haircut entered and walked to the barber at the closest chair and extended his hand. "Good afternoon, my name is Rex Buford. What's yours?" The barber answered and shook the man's hand. The new customer did this at each chair. Novel, to say the least. When he had met all the barbers he asked, "Do I need an appointment?" He was told no. "Good" he said, "and how much for a shave and a haircut?"

"Shave and a haircut...six bits," came the answer. It was melodic.

A scissors fell into a sink with an ear-splitting rattle-rattle and an electric trimmer fell to the floor with a troubling kerklank-kerklank. All barbering stopped. Do I really have to tell you who sang the classic response? I daren't think so. I will anyway. It was the bozo who has "heard 'em all."

Proofreading

In the literary field there is no professional pursuit more useful and honorable than the proofreader. He, or she, stands as the last line of defense against the unwelcomed misspelling, the out-of-place punctuation, the typographical car wreck. When proofread, the manuscript goes "to press" for subsequent delivery to you, the reader. No one else sees it until you do. Okay, the pressman does, but he's just making sure that the reds are red and the blues are blue. Some of them can't even read so I've noticed. You, the reader, benefit by gliding through the written message corrected of any miscues. Your reading enjoyment is enhanced by a verbal highway with no potholes, no detours, no traffic jams.

There was a time, I confess, when this writer did not hold the proof-reader in the high esteem that the profession deserves. With the advent of the computer and spell-check software, I held the opinion that proofreaders had become obsolete.

In retrospect (following hand-holding counseling from other staffers who were around at the time) I decided that some of the things I said at the Christmas party that year I needed to disavow. A little too much from the holiday nog bowl apparently – no, reportedly – set me off in a dialogue direc-tion about proofreaders I came to regret.

All in all I think it is water under the bridge, over the dam even. The head of the proofreading team has proved to be an understanding fellow. I salute him and appreciate his forbearing in the face of some of my comments. I made a mistake about him when I was under the impression he was a woman. I'll not say it was merely a mistake anyone might have made after several glasses from that festive punch bowl. No, it was my mistake and I admit it freely.

Now when we pass in the hall or see each other in an elevator we can acknowl-edge a new bond of togetherness between author and proofreader. We speak on these occasions and I can sense that the past is past and any old grievances are buried. With this new fraternity between us, I gladly say that writers can confi-dently turn their "scribblings" over to this highly qualified last line of defenders.

Let me just say that I do continue to use the computer's spelling review feature, but only because, as I have said before, I sometimes get confused over some words. Nevertheless I reiterate that the clean, error-absent Ob-servations I write, such as this one, arrive within your ken only after the careful and expert rendering of the proofreading corps.

Moving on I have a few important remarks to make about

(Yeah, right. Proofreaders aren't stupid, Mr. Ob. We have long memories and the last say about your idiotic typescripts. We also have the last review to make changes and additions… and the last laugh. See you around, dirtbag. What kind of a name is Ob anyway?)

The History Ob-servations

(John Thom writes:)

There is a rich lode in the history books for Constantinople Ob to mine to bring new insights into our past. We include these in this special closing section.

1492

Oh, yeah, sure, Christopher Columbus changed the landscape by his daring explorations across unknown reaches of sea to a land without European footprints. We learned this in elementary school from history books. And rhymes. Remember "In 1492 Columbus sailed the ocean blue..."? And the famous trio of sailing vessels, the Nina, the Pinta and the Santa Maria?

Well, history books aside and rhymes notwithstanding, there's more to the story. Ole Chris set out with a quartet of boats. Those three we've all heard about plus his own favorite, the "Ace of Spades." Seems the dauntless seaman was a bit of a joy rider. The A of S was a sleek 3-masted caravelle capable of 20-25 leagues a day if under full sails and on a favorable sea. Columbus turned the Ace of Spades over to a close pal, also an Italian. Chris was an Italian, a Genovian to be more specific. Italians like speed.

The crew of the A of S was special, too. Men of bottomless appetites for fun, frolic and festive ways. They could wear out a day's agenda of work and play. More play than work. What is there to do out in the middle of nowhere anyway? Follow orders? Yes, of course. When it pleased them, and that's where the path of history veered. Columbus was more goal-oriented than the men of the A of S turned out to be.

Alongside one day, Chris, on board one of his obedient boats, cautioned his buddies on the A of S to "heave to" in the honored way of disciplined seamanship leading to their shared mission of discovery. They were on their way to India. It was a rhetorical shot across the bow of the Ace of Spades.

"What if we don't want to?" someone shouted, parrying the thrust of the boss's wishes.

"Shiver me timbers," Chris said, surely feeling this was the justifiable, though agonizing, response to a challenge to his authority.

The Nina, the Pinta, the Santa Maria and the Ace of Spades all sailed under the flag of Spain. The crews comprised experienced seagoing Spaniards, Italians, Portuguese, and French cooks. Columbus spoke only Italian. But he had good hearing. He heard a squeaky, higher-than-expected pitch to a voice. "Are there any women on the Ace of Spades?" he asked in an exasperated tone as his own boat bobbed near the A of S, he struggling to re-assert his command. "Did I just hear a woman's voice?"

"So what if you did?" came a sneering answer. "You've got your own on your boat."

"I…most…certainly…do…not," Chris shouted. True perhaps but that didn't win any points in the argument with the, uh, broad-minded sailors on the Ace of Spades.

"We didn't plan to come all this way just to sail off the edge of the earth without some distraction," another seaman gleefully yelled from the A of S.

There was no mistaking that Chris received this rejoinder as if punched in the stomach. How could they believe this was the accepted doctrine of ocean exploration? "The world is not flat," he retorted back to the A of S crew members…and memberettes.

"How do you know? Seen different?"

Whereupon Christopher Columbus sculpted a dazzlingly brilliant description of the earth as a sphere around which a boat, even one as mischievous as the Ace of Spades, could start a voyage in a port in any country and sail the seven seas without fear of disappearing and then venture right back into the same port, proof positive the world was round. The lecture took almost ten minutes as he hollered through the winds and tumbling sea. The guys and gals on the A of S listened for about the first 30 seconds.

It was also the last ten minutes that the intrepid Christopher Columbus searched for undiscovered lands – or any, for that matter – with four boats. The Ace of Spades lowered its Spanish colors, wheeled south and headed to the edge of the earth. It got there, too, but it did not fall off. The Ace of Spades navigated its way into an expansive river delta, stopped for lack of fulfilling winds, and established a settlement.

Operating under the powerful forces in the DNA passed through generations of their uppity ancestors, the French cooks stiffened their resolve and their backs, telling the crewmen of the A of S that there would be no more Gallic cuisine unless they – the French cooks – could christen the settlement. The eclectic crew – and their cooperative companionettes – could not have cared less and easily agreed. And New Orleans came to be.

Columbus went on to discover America. In turn, America discovered European germs, repression and other bad habits.

A Word Interlude

I was re-reading *Word for Word*, our amazing dictionary, and came across this entry, which I have always thought was pretty terrific:

"Assemble, v. – To put parts from different sources together to make a whole as opposed to manufacturing everything for the product in one place. Airplanes and cars are made this way and quite successfully. So was the universe over a 6-day sequence."

We know God assembled things – and did not manufacture the parts – because she is really smart. By herself she would not have built man with so many imperfections. She "made" man on the sixth day of her busy week. As man is created in God's image, we must also assume that the plans she handed over to the subcontractors were, unfortunately, pretty sketchy. They must have shown only the skeleton because the final product takes lots of liberties with the presumed God-look-alike idea; man comes in too many different shapes, colors, heights, weights and attitudes, oh, and different opinions. Lots of different opinions.

Upon seeing the results, God decided to summon her chief design engineer. She asked her office assistant (OA), "Who is responsible for this mess? Get me what's-his-name." When what's-his-name appeared, she said, "Just what is your name?"

He answered, "Beelzebub."

"Well, Bee, I'm disappointed with your work. Look at man!"

"What's wrong with him…and her?"

"It's a mess, a disaster. I don't know if it can be fixed. Where were you when it was being built, asleep?"

"I'm an archangel, I don't have to take this from you or anyone."

"You'll take it from me today, and you'll like it."

"Jesus Christ!" he snapped.

"Watch your tongue," she countered.

"Why? There's no law against saying that."

"There will be."

"What's the problem here anyway?"

"It was supposed to be created in my image, and just look."

"That's not my fault. Your plans were very preliminary, just a bunch of bones, then you said to be sure we used only the low bidders. Do you know what kind of quality we get out of those job shops over in Nod? And these angels you told me to use on the production line. They're hopeless, always whining about something. Did you know they're talking about forming a union?"

"That's as may be. By the way, who in hell told you to install free will? That's just not going to work."

"Who in where? Hell? What's that?"

"You'll learn about that soon enough, too. By the way, where did you field test man?"

"In Eden."

"Eden!?!? What kind of test is that? It's got everything they could possibly want. There's nothing there that would present them with any challenge. How will we know if it can cope if it doesn't face some challenges or choices?"

"(Cough) There is this apple tree."

"Apple tree? Are you mocking me?" Then she calmed down. "Tell me what happened."

"It's in my report. I call it Genesis."

"All right. Leave it on my desk on your way out. And one last thing, go to hell…and send my OA in." The OA passed Beelzebub on her way in and his way out…to the nether region. "Yes, your Supremeness?"

"Get me Mother Nature. I've got to talk to her about global warming. What? Oh, okay, climate change. I'm tired. Cancel all my appointments for tomorrow, I really need to take a day off."

The First Thanksgiving

In a clearing in a wooded grove not far apart from their sleeping huts, the Puritan souls dug several fire pits to roast the fowls they had gathered for the feast. Their intent was, like their faith, humble. It was to give thanks to their God for the beneficence they were enjoying in the New World. It was the First Thanksgiving. (I know, a grove is automatically "wooded." Relax, please.)

How the First Thanksgiving ever got to a second one has stumped the best paleontologists and archaeologists since 1621.

Naturally, at a feast that suspended the usual hard work for a day, the kids raised riot as soon as the sun cracked through the pines. The dust they kicked up competed with the aroma of the turkeys browning on spits over the fire pits. "Stop that screaming and stop that running," the children were admonished every five minutes. "Why don't you behave like your older brothers and sisters?" More admonishment, this time in the form of behavioral advice.

Of course, if they had taken that advice, the younger children would be out of sight in amongst the trees playing slap and tickle or spin the bottle. Puritan veniality, apparently. Studying surviving diaries from this period reveals that the teens adopted these games on the boats sailing over from the old country. Atlantic crossings would be tedious without a few diverting amusements was the consensus of the archaeologists.

The women. The poor women. Stereotypically thrust into the role as cooks. Hours plucking the feathers from the turkeys and disemboweling them of slimy innards. Bartering with one another to pull together a few spices to baste into the dead birds.

In these conditions it would easily take eight or ten hours to bring a fowl to table-ready. If they had tables. "How hard is it to make a table?" Hester asked. Millicent nodded her head. Virginia, who was "married" to the carpenter, snapped, "He doesn't have all his tools, you know." Millicent, snickering, nodded her head again. Hester laughed. "Oh, please," Virginia said angrily, "and I suppose that drudge of a smithy of yours hasn't had a whack or two on his head?" "Don't go down that road again," Millicent shouted. Only seven more hours until dinnertime.

The men, Puritan to the bone, assembled out of earshot to hold an ad hoc bible study. They took as their verse the uplifting story of Susannah and the Elders, she who faced impure machinations of the two conspiring and eavesdropping judges while she took the sun in her garden after a reviving bath, her shoulders undraped for the warmth, her blouse undone where her long hair could not cover her billowing beauty, her tunic opened giving freedom to her legs. The men examined the lesson at some length…and depth.

The men, in their discussion, appeared to take some major liberties with the text of their quite new King James version of the bible, liberties that included readings not even included by the king. That story about the tart, er, the victim, Susannah, for example, is excised from most bibles owing to its questionable authorship. It did not deter these fellows.

"Hey, William, where'd you come by this book? It's not in my bible, and I've looked for it," one of the men asked William. "Yeah, I thought it was contraband," another piped in to William. William answered, "Can you believe that summer we just went through? I'm wondering what our winters are going to be like."

"Josephus," yelled one of the women, "it's time for supper." Shaken from their theological meditations about poor Susannah, the men wandered back to the clearing. Also arriving was a band of about twenty barely clothed men, women and children. "Oh, my suffering iliac, who invited the bloody Indians?" someone gasped.

A Lien On America

Before the rabble-rousing American upstarts tweaked the noses of their British landlords in 1776, a covey of envoys sailed to England with the aim of re-financing the mortgage King George the Third held on the new-world colonies. Taxes and such and the ornery attitude displayed at every turn by the redcoats had combined to push the colonial subjects to a feisty edge.

"Let's at least," some of the infuriated Americans urged, "get lower interest rates." Surely, the argument went at the time, Mad George will recognize and then ease the usurious hold he has on the properties along the east coast of the continent. Representatives from Philadelphia, New York, Providence, Boston, etc., nodded their heads in agreement. A commission of envoys was formed.

The mission is a little-known foray into foreign relations by the usually passive citizens who were typically modest merchants, farmers and small businessmen. Because it was an utter failure, the mission is skipped over by the history books, which go straight on to the more glamorous exploits on the battlefields of the Revolutionary War.

A bon-voyage party of about twenty people – wives and children of the envoys – stood on the dock below the gangplank of a tri-masted sailing vessel to wave goodbye. Today, they could board a jumbo jet and fly in comparative comfort across the Atlantic in about five or six hours. Not in the 18th century. What they got then was weeks of bone-jarring interaction with ocean swells, storms, seasickness, crappy rations, endless tedium, dysentery, pointless debates with the dumber members of the commission, and a disheartening preview of the equally appalling sailing back to America awaiting them once their mission in England was completed.

If the captain and the helmsman and navigator were any good, the boat would find a convenient port in southern England fairly easily. If they weren't drunk. Okay, luck was on their side. As to the American passengers, if the mission leader had planned ahead, they would have had comfortable rooms in, say, Southampton for a few days of lodging so they could regain their land legs.

"Was I supposed to reserve rooms? Was that my job?" This was the unfortunate and unacceptable reaction by their leader. It was bad enough the commission had to settle for cheap lodgings, four to a dirty room and English food, but did they have to share quarters with the same uncouth sailors from their boat?

Southampton is about twenty leagues southwest of London. Geography courses in American schools in the 18th century did not teach that. "Where then is the king?" the envoys asked each other. They all went to American schools where that answer also was not taught. Locals who went to English schools know the answer – "some castle in London."

What the locals did not know was how to get to "some castle in London." What happened in London was of no concern to the locals in south England. Many things had not yet been invented, such as trains, buses, cars, and regional jets, conveyances, which lacking, meant the locals stayed local and the American envoys would have sold their souls to use. Instead, the envoys had to overpay for a few horse-drawn coaches, horse droppings, muddy roads and all.

"The stink and squalor and crowds of human despair we find in London gives us pause," one of the envoys wrote in a diary. Accommodations in the great city were almost identical to the ones the envoys rented in Southampton. The big difference was no sailors in the rooms. There would have been no room for the sailors as the beds not used by the envoys were used by Irishmen. Almost as bad.

Weeks of sea agonies and days of English inhospitality meant the commission was closer to its objective, i.e., a mortgage re-financing session with his majesty, King George the Third.

"Where does the king live?" the envoys inquired.

"The king?"

"Yes, the king."

"Wherever he damn well pleases," came the answer.

"Where does he live right now?"

"Right now?"

"Yes, right now."

"In Paris."

"In Paris?"

"Yes, in Paris."

"What is he doing in Paris?"

"Whatever he damn well pleases."

"But we have to meet with him."

"Who are you?"

"We are the mortgage re-finance commission from the American colonies delegated by our fellow citizens to seek redress from the usurious financial burdens on our homes and businesses."

"Oh."

This is a reasonably accurate account of the sadly fruitless trip by the envoys to re-fi American mortgages. Perhaps its brevity of drama and shortage of success is the determining factor as to why the trip is not celebrated in the same breath as the Boston Tea Party or Concord and Lexington or Valley Forge or Paul Revere's ride. Makes sense.

A Key And A Kite

If you ask me, this is how it happened way back when in Philadelphia.

"Honey," he said from another room, "have you got a key?"

"Yes," she said also from another room. Moments passed.

"Honey, have you got a key?" (Said a little louder.)

"Yes." (Said a little more determinedly.) A short moment passed.

"Where is it?"

"Where is what?"

"Your key."

"I'm not sure. Why do you want to know if I have a key? Are you locked out?"

"No. I want it."

"Whatever for if you are not locked out?"

"I want to take it outside."

"In this weather? There's a mighty storm out there."

"I know. That's why."

"You're not making sense."

"I plan to put it onto my kite and fly it up into the storm."

"*Now* you are making sense." (She was being sarcastic.)

"I want to see what happens when the lightning comes and hits the key. I think I'll discover something important."

"Uh-huh. And what is that then?"

"I can't say now. I'll know when the time comes."

"So you want to go out in a frightening storm and fly a kite with a key on it?"

"Yes."

"Has it occurred to you what the neighbors will say? Some of them already believe you to be a loon."

"What they think of me is of no consequence."

"Perhaps, but what they think of me depends a great deal on what they think of you. Think of me."

"They'll get over it when I tell them just how important this is."

"They're going to think much better of you, then me, after you tell them you are going to fly a kite with my key on it in a barnburner of a storm? I'd like to hear that explanation."

"I told you, it's going to..."

"Wait. Let me finish wiping the dishes before you explain this."

"I'm in a hurry. I don't know how long this storm will be kicking up the way it is. The lightning may pass by."

"Hold your horses. I'll be there in a jiffy."

A jiffy passed.

"Okay, the dishes are done, no thanks to you, and I've made myself a nice cup of tea. Do you want a cup?"

"No."

"It'd warm you. You know it's pretty stormy out tonight and it's very cold."

"Yes, I know, that's what I've been saying right along."

"Okay, if that's how you feel. Now what's this silliness you have in your head?"

"It's not silli...oh, never mind. Here's what it is. I fly the kite with a key on it and a stroke of lightning smacks into it."

"Won't that ruin the kite? I mean the whole thing will fall to the ground."

"Maybe. But what I expect is that the lightning will hit the key. It's made of iron and I believe it will attract the lightning. I think it will demonstrate how the static electricity we see in our lab experiments is the same as the bolts produced in storms."

"Uh-huh. And with that our neighbors are going to say that you are not a loon?" (She was being sarcastic again.)

"Never mind about them."

"If you're so keen on discovering something that people will admire you for, why not find a way to warm our house better than that old fireplace? Something practical. A nice stove. You could call it, oh, I don't know, a Benjamin Burner."

"One thing at a time. Now, where's that key?"

"Over there on the cupboard. Don't lose it and don't let it get bent when the lightning hits it. It won't be worth anything then."

"Okay. Where's my galoshes?"

"Do I have to find everything?"

Stowaway

Sometimes don't you just wonder? You see something or you hear something or you read something and you just wonder. I do, and that's what happened to me recently. It was a headline in one of those newspapers at the checkout counter at the grocery store. I don't remember the exact headline. It was something like "Paris Police Suspect Stowaway on the Spirit of St. Louis."

Don't you just wonder? Sure you do. Maybe not before, but you do now. You have several things to wonder about. I'll readily admit that I have and I did. I wondered about several things about a stowaway on the Spirit of St. Louis.

What I wonder about is where the guy was sitting when the plane took off. I mean the pilot would have noticed right away if he had a passenger in the seat next to him. (It was not a big airplane.)

"Good morning, sir, do you have your boarding pass?" is not the first thing the pilot would have had on his mind. I'm sure he would have said, "Hey, what are you doing here?" Or he could have said, "Hey, where do you think you're going?" Of course that second response would have been a dead end. Everyone knew where the Spirit of St. Louis was going. What I would have said was, "Sir, please get off this plane." Forthrightness is called for in a ticklish situation. Besides which, stowaways always hide under a blanket or a tarpaulin or behind a life raft or in a laundry chute. The whole idea of a stowaway is to be undetected. It's the amateur stowaway who doesn't know this.

Then I wondered did the stowaway have the presence of mind to pack a lunch. If it were me, I'd include a sandwich, probably something like beef or ham or tuna along with an apple and maybe a cookie. Something to drink, too. I'd be careful not to put my lunch items in those noisy aluminum wrappers. It'd give me away as soon as I started to eat. Don't take this the wrong way. I am not a stowaway and I have never been a stowaway. I also have no plans to become a stowaway.

All this just makes you wonder, doesn't it? Then I wondered if the stowaway made himself known to the pilot after they had been in the air for a while. Like what would he say.

"Ahem."

"What?!?!"

"I said ahem."

"Not what did you say. What the heck are you doing here?"

"Not much. There's hardly any room to do anything."

"You're not supposed to be here."

"I know. That's why we're called stowaways."

"How did you...where were...what are...?"

"Sorry to be a bother."

"Sorry to be a bother? Are you out of your mind? Do you know what you've done? Oh, my stars. This is a disaster."

"Oh, don't be nervous. I won't cause any trouble."

"Trouble? Not cause trouble? You already have. Do you know what I am doing?"

"Well, yes, it's kinda obvious."

"Is it? Is it obvious? What is it that's so obvious?"

"You're flying an airplane. I'm right, no?"

"That's it? That is what is so obvious to you? Nothing else?"

"Gosh, no. Am I missing something?"

"Is he missing something? Try this on for size. I am flying across the Atlantic Ocean. I will be the first to fly solo across that ocean."

"Honest? That is keen. The first. No one has done this before? I didn't know that. Keen."

"You're still missing it, aren't you?"

"Missing what?"

"The essential point."

"I'm afraid you've got me there. I suppose I am missing something. I give up. Tell me."

"Great guns! Where to begin. I know, I'll begin at the end."

"That's novel."

"Shut up."

"Righto."

"Shut up. Okay. I get to the end of this flight and I step out of the airplane to be greeted by a throng of people who will cheer my achievement. The first person to fly solo across the Atlantic Ocean."

"Cheers well deserved, I say."

"Shut up. When I get out of the airplane as the first person to fly solo across the Atlantic Ocean, it is going to be somewhat invalidating when a second person gets out of the same airplane. Two people in an airplane on a solo flight is likely to raise questions. Someone there is certain to ask me if I understood the rules."

"Oh."

"Makes you wonder, doesn't it?"

"It certainly does. You'll be mortified."

"Yes, mortified, unless I land alone."

"Ooh. I get your drift. Wait, I read you as a pacifistic type. There must be another avenue."

"I cannot think of one."

"Ooh."

The Challenge

No one knows how long he held the title. There were no official records and the anecdotal evidence was skimpy and unreliable. No one came forward to claim otherwise, so the populace was satisfied that the tortoise wore the belt legitimately. After all, he did defeat the hare.

The hare. The embarrassment. His anguish. The stupefied look upon his face on the day in question. The moral – often forgotten today – he begat. Such is the hare's legacy. Veterinary biologists who tried to rationalize the hare's race performance studied his species with care. The circumference of his brain in ratio to the length of his spinal column was found to be tinier than in any other animal save the dinosaur. The dinosaur, however, presented a disadvantage to the geometry, owing to its exceedingly long body. That length seemed to be a bit of overkill if you ask me.

Die-hard supporters of the hare raised a ruckus over that laboratory study – brains and spines – and demanded the vets also measure the tortoise to see how it stacked up ratio-wise. They overlooked one thing, though. Turtles have shells and you can't see their spines. Hare supporters did not think that one out at all. Wonder what *their* ratios are.

The foot race between the tortoise and the hare is not the first one we know about. The first foot race belongs to a time prior when Abel was unable to out-gain Cain.

The turtle's victory over the hare certainly had plenty of notoriety associated with it as foot racing became quite popular and continues up to our own time. Yes, today's foot racers are very competent and the contests would rank higher in favor among sporting fans were it not for the over-commercialization attached to it. And let's not bring up steroids.

So it was with a strong whiff of excitement when a new challenge was issued to the tortoise. Another race. To be held in the amateur tradition. Mano a mano. No prize money, just the satisfaction of victory upon effort. Oh, and that champion's belt, too.

Sidling up one day a snail said, "Wanna race?" There it was. The challenge!

Let's be honest here and admit that the tortoise was amused. "Oh, come now," he said dismissively.

"Whatsa matter," the snail inquired, "you a chicken?"

"It would be a bit one-sided, wouldn't you say?" the tortoise figured.

"How's that?" the snail asked.

The tortoise tried to explain by analogy when he said, "The only thing slower than you is a reform bill moving through Congress."

Snails are quicker on the uptake than you may want to admit. He said, "Look, you jerk, a while back you knocked off a hare – a consummately stupid hare to be sure but a hare nonetheless – and he was a million times swifter than you. What makes you think I would not have a chance?" The tortoise made no answer. "Hey!" yelled the snail, "are you alive?"

The tortoise stirred. "Sorry, I was reminiscing."

"What-ever," the snail belched, "you gonna race me or not?"

"Okay."

As neither participant had anything else to do they settled on tomorrow for the race. Actually, tomorrow night for the obvious reason. "I am a mollusk of the class gastropod," the snail explained, "so I cannot compete in the daytime. The sun would turn me into a prune."

"A mollusk? Ugh," the turtle responded, adding boastfully and one-upping his challenger, "I am a reptile of the order Chelonia and that makes me better than you. Heck, almost every living thing is better than you, but, in fairness, I would except the scorpion." The snail stared back at the turtle and under his breath said, "Ass."

Tomorrow arrived and the starting time for the challenge was established. The course was described. The water stations were set at intervals. The crowd was petitioned to remain back away from the competitors to ensure safety. The belt was on display. As dark settled, the race began. There was no moon out to light the course.

At the finish line, a snail of the same size, shape and demeanor as the challenger waited out of sight of the race officials and spectators. It was his job to slip surreptitiously onto the course ahead of the tortoise and break the tape while behind him the challenger himself, equally surreptitiously, was slipping into nearby bushes.

Two things are instructive to know about this. One, the snail's brain circumference ratio to his spine was pretty positive, putting him in a position to outthink the turtle, and, two, it was night, my friends, so nobody could detect the skullduggery that was being fashioned.

Moral: Slow and steady may win the race when it is an obtuse hare you are up against, as Aesop claimed, but cheating in the dark is just a plain sure-fire tactic.

Newton And The Apple

Newton, he's sitting under an apple tree on an enviable fall day in the 17th century minding his own business, reading a book maybe or writing haiku when out of somewhere, thunk!, an apple hits him square on the head. He exclaims, "What in the holy heck is that all about, huh?"

Apple tree, apple, head exposed, whop! This man Newton was no slouch. He knew just what was called for. Running from the orchard, he went hurriedly through the farmhouse door calling, "Isaac, Isaac, come here, will you? I was just attacked by an apple."

Isaac, inside because that is where his books and instruments and experiments were strewn, replied, "Brother, brother, stay calm, it might just be only an…"

Here, Isaac's brother – the history books I have examined do not record Isaac's serendipitous brother's name, so I shall christen him, oh, Ichabod – Ichabod interrupts to finish Isaac's thought. "…an example of the treachery of that Cromwell clan next door. They were throwing apples at me, I am certain, spot on upon my head. There can be no other explanation."

Isaac said, "Wait one, Ich, I am going to enter into profound contemplation to see what I might fathom from your experience. It's what I do as you know. You were in our orchard under an apple tree and an apple hit you on the head and you claim misdemeanant behavior by our neighbors." "Yeah," Ich said.

Isaac thought. (Remember, thinking was a favorite activity of his.) He thought: apple tree, Ich, apple, ouch! Cromwell clan. That's the testimony. It might be illuminating to re-enact the episode, Isaac mused, but that would mean enlisting the participation of those Cromwell slugs, a trio of intolerable bullies if ever there was to be one. Isaac, like Ich, didn't care for the Cromwell boys, a position they held with everyone else in the shire. "Dang, and I so like experimenting," Isaac said.

"On the other hand," he considered, "I could cross-examine Ich to validate that what he said happened actually did happen." Clever as he was, and having had experience with Ich and Ich's sometimes unreliable recollecting of events, Isaac took what he believed would be an instructive preliminary step prior to his re-examination of Ich's apple orchard episode. They would talk later.

Later came. Isaac and Ich convened in the orchard below the very tree where Ich was targeted. "Here?" Isaac asked. "Yeah," Ich answered. "Sitting?" Isaac asked. "Yeah," Ich answered. "On top of your head?" Isaac asked. "Yeah, and it scared me," Ich answered. "Where were the Cromwell boys?" Isaac asked. "Don't know, didn't see them," Ich answered.

"There is a reason you didn't see them, Ich, and that is that they were nowhere around to be seen." Isaac explained things to Ich as the saga moved irrevocably toward an electric and historic moment of discovery. "Not around?" Ich said with surprise. "Not around," Isaac replied, "they were all day that day over in Borplestreamshire visiting some family members who are not entirely put off by the three boys."

Ich was mortified. "I was sure it was those slugs," he said.

Isaac responded, "Not all observations prove to be without some flaws." (Editor's note: This comment ought not to be taken as an evaluation of the Ob-servations by our own C. Ob.)

Ich thought for a moment, not to the depths of his famous brother, but with some useful productivity in this case. "That can mean only one thing then," Ich cried, "and that is that I just discovered gravity."

Now Isaac was mortified. In his mind he read, "Ich…discovery…gravity." He blanched. "Why didn't I think of that? That's my job."

Ich looked at his favorite brother. "Not to worry, Isaac, I'll let you have it as your own. I owe you anyway for not telling mom that time I lit the barn on fire."

Isaac nodded. "Don't remind me. That was when I should have taken account of the thermodynamic effects of your arson and when I could have written another award-winning paper. And I didn't. But *c'est la vie.*"

Evolution?

Charles Darwin may have got it right. There's some pretty fair evidence fish grew legs, formed nostrils, waded ashore, and invested in beachfront property before prices went sky high.

A look at some of the mansions dotting almost any coast will tell us, convincingly, that slimy creatures from the sea have been naturally selected into something approximating homeowners. That was in the Pre-Cambrian epoch. There is no video evidence because there were no video cams, which means no visual record.

In the Cambrian period, prices stabilized when zoning commissions packed with NIMBYs put restrictions on high-rise developments. Suburbs sprouted everywhere putting pressure on prices. Some birds morphed into dinosaurs, or maybe it was the other way round.

In the Ordovician interlude, local nines played pickup games on Saturdays just for the heck of it. Wives and children attended more out of loyalty than for the level of accomplishment demonstrated by the sides. Umpires were frequently razzed.

From hence came the Silurian, Devonian, Carboniferous, Permian, Triassic and Jurassic periods, or epochs. It would be unfair to say nothing much happened unless we knew the facts. We don't, so if anything much did happen, well, it doesn't show up in any chronicles uncovered up to now. We might speculate. That's always a kick. There could have been earthquakes to help form continents. A meteor or two might have plunked Earth upside its head. There was probably at least one Ice Age. (They made a movie about it.) And didn't that shut up the global warming crackpots of the day. Then when the planet began warming again, who went running to the hills? *Tempus fugit* and *caveat emptor*, I guess

Whereupon we find ourselves in the Cretaceous and Tertiary eras, two periods chock-a-block with exciting change and unlimited adventure. Take as just one example the Great Flood, or The Deluge, when it rained a reported forty days and forty nights. From it came a boatload (pun intended) of water all around. Owing to a fortuitous conversation regarding laying keels and how long is a cubit and who are compatible pairs, a man built the Ark. You've heard of it, right? The titanic vessel commissioned by God, constructed by Noah, staffed by nepotism, launched in a notorious rainstorm and bound for Ararat. The passengers were couples only and every couple wishing to sail had to declare its heterosexuality. For reasons no one can explain today, the manifest included two cockroaches, two piranhas, and an Italian man.

The idea behind the boat was "save the animals." The idea behind The Deluge is anybody's guess. Oh, and forty days and forty nights of non-stop rain? People in Seattle still get a laugh out of that. "Forty? That's no more than a light shower," they might say.

Then we reach the Quaternary stage. That's ours. We're in it now. And what has evolution brought us? Computers that can calculate the numerical value of pi out to millions of digits past the decimal, but cannot boot up when you are in a hurry. Telephones that can carry voices with amazing clarity around the world, but cannot prevent sales calls from home remodelers at dinner time. Weathermen who can foresee isobars for thousands of miles, but who fail to notice when they have to use their windshield wipers. Scientists who can describe and illustrate fifteen billion years of the Big Bang explosion and the ensuing shrapnel known as galaxies, but who cannot tell us who lit the fuse to cause the initial event. And acne.

The Big Purchase

Let us set the record straight about something. Something important. No, I don't want your nominations, I already have the important something to make a straight record of.

It started at the front door. Knock-knock. "I'll get it, Thom," Sally said jumping off his lap. She scampered – patter, patter, patter – down the stairway and across the hall to the door. "Are you expecting anyone today?" she called back before answering the knock.

"No, could be anyone, I suppose," Thom answered.

"I'll see," Sally said unnecessarily but cordially and servilely.

"Yes'm, who be that?" Sally shifted tones when she opened the door, bowing a little to a woman in about her mid-twenties and clutching a rucksack filled, it turned out, with a load of paperwork.

"Is the man of the house in?" the woman asked, looking past Sally into the foyer.

"Whas this all abou?" Sally said, shuffling a bit.

"The man of the house. I wish to speak with him about a business matter."

"He awful busy, you know, runnin thins," Sally said, trying not to look the woman in her eyes.

"That's fine, girl, I won't take much of his time."

"Yes'm. Step in. Whas yo name?"

"Tell him it is Miranda Milck. Milck with a 'c'."

"Yes'm." Sally went back upstairs. "There is a white woman downstairs, Thom, who says she wants to talk with you about a business matter. She said her name is Miranda Milck. She says it is Milck with a 'c.' Shall I bring her up?"

"No, Sal. Show her into the parlor. I will be there presently."

"I will brew tea for the two of you."

"Thank you, Sal."

After a few moments, the man of the house arrived at the parlor door. "Miss Milck, hello, how may I help you?"

"It is Mrs. Milck, and you are?"

"Jefferson, Thomas Jefferson."

"Jefferson. That sounds familiar. Have you been in Virginia long?"

"Oh yes, for many years."

"My office manager did not tell me that. Well anyway, Mr. Jefferson, I am in the real estate business. I am canvassing Charlottesville because I have some very attractive properties coming on the market, and the way things are going in our country, people seem to want more land."

"Uh-huh."

"You and your wife have a beautiful estate here, I must say. What…"

"Excuse me. I have no wife, Mrs. Milck. I am a widower these many years."

"Oh, I see. I see. Your estate here, what do you call it?"

"Monticello."

"How charming. You had an artistic architect to be sure."

"In reality, Mrs. Milck, I am responsible for most of the design."

"Are you. You must be a very clever chap." (In an adjacent room, Sally, eavesdropping, laughed at that comment.) "Have you thought," Mrs. Milck went on, "about relocating from…oh no, you wouldn't, not from this gorgeous plantation."

"That is fair to say," Jefferson admitted, "but the fact is that I have been considering acquiring more land. My colleagues are pressing me to do just that."

"Oh, the boys down at the tavern, yes? You farmers are always looking for more soil to till." Mrs. Milck was getting excited. A prospective buyer. "It just so happens, Mr. Jefferson, that I have a parcel of forty acres just a few miles down the road toward Waynesboro. The seller is anxious to turn it loose, and I think he would be willing to let it go for under…"

"Uh, Mrs. Milck, I was thinking of something larger than forty acres."

"All right, yes, good, yes, larger than forty acres, very good. The Wilson brothers could be talked into selling that hundred-acre spread down toward Lynchburg. It…"

"Again, Mrs. Milck, something larger than one hundred acres."

Mrs. Milck stared at Mr. Jefferson and calculated. "Not forty," she said to herself, "not one hundred." She thumbed through her papers. "Well, here is one that is considerably larger. The seller is a French gentleman goes by the name of, uh, let me look, uh, yes, Napoleon Bonaparte. He's just listed the property. He said he needs some cash to settle some affairs in Europe."

"Where is the property?" Jefferson inquired.

"It is west from here. It runs from the lower Mississippi Valley out toward the Rocky Mountains. Lots of grassland it says here, waterways, room to do whatever tickles your fancy."

"How large is it?"

"It is, it is right here, let me…okay, here. It is, my oh my, it is five hundred and twenty million acres. That's more than the Wilson's hundred-acre plot," Mrs. Milck joked.

"What is Mr. Bonaparte asking for this property?"

"The price, yes, also right here in…oh yes, here it is. It is sixty million francs. I don't know how much that is in real money, Mr. Jefferson, but I can ask over to the bank and they can tell us how much it will be in U.S. specie. Does this sound like something you and your friends would be interested in, Mr. Jefferson?"

"I have had my eye out for something around that size, yes. My friends in Washington think we should be looking to expand and west is the right direction to be looking."

"Oh, you know people in Washington, do you? Maybe they can help. You could form a real estate investment trust and pool your money and spread the risk and get this Mr. Bonaparte to, um, part with the property. By the way, he will want cash. He says his creditors in Europe won't settle for…"

"I can get the cash, Mrs. Milck. I know a money man in Washington."

"A rich millionaire, is he? That is always a helpful acquaintance to have when you are buying land. Cash money talks."

"He is the Treasurer of the United States."

"Oh, a big shot. Even better. Next you will tell me you know the president," Mrs. Milck laughed. "But seriously, I will have my office draw up the property transfer contracts. They will open an escrow account and find an exterminator to tent the property for termites. If you want, we can have a survey crew go out there and determine where the property lines are. It starts down in the Mississippi Delta near New Orleans and runs all the way up to Canada."

"No need for that, Mrs. Milck, I will establish my own lines. Maybe next year I will send an exploration team out there. I have the authority. I know a couple of guys."

"Excellent. That will save a long trip for my survey crew, and I admire your executive aptitude." (In that adjacent room, Sally, still eavesdropping, was still laughing.)

"Won't we need a really big tent to kill all the termites, Mrs. Milck?" Jefferson said.

"Why yes, I suppose we will," she said, missing the humor. "Now if I can have just a little bit more information about you, Mr. Jefferson, for the escrow papers. You know, to keep the record straight. Let's start with your occupation."

Ptolemy Or Copernicus

It's one thing to look up into the heavens today and make jokes about Flat Earthists and moon-landing conspiracy adherents and the folks who still believe the sun revolves around the earth. Fortunately, advances in scientific methodology and the arrival of television have pretty much settled these questions to most people's satisfaction. Sure, pockets of doubt still persist. For example, North Koreans still believe the sun shines out Kim's backside. And what a backside it is.

These were not always laughing matters. Take Ptolemy. Around two thousand years ago he carefully and painstakingly described how the sun and all that other space debris revolves around our planet. Nobody laughed at him. Maybe at his silly name, but not at his "geocentric theory." The evidence was clear to him. Every morning the sun appeared in the east, passed along a predictable course above Ptolemy and disappeared in the west. Nothing funny about that. Case closed.

For the next one thousand, four hundred years or so, school children got patted on their heads when they answered the question "How does the universe work?" with "Ptolemy's way."

Then along comes Copernicus who says, "Stupid kids." Rhetorically speaking, that is. He was more polite than that. Maybe he said, "You are so wrong, children." He then proceeds to carefully and painstakingly describe how Earth and selected other space debris circle the sun. His "heliocentric theory." Loads of people laughed at him because there was something funny about his theory. The claims against him went on the lines of, "You are so dumb. Go re-read Ptolemy."

Ptolemy or Copernicus. Copernicus or Ptolemy. Competing treatises on a consequential question. You had to take sides. It was an either/or situation. Research by your correspondent discovered there were no cable news networks on the air back in the 16th century to host a discussion panel to declare a victor. Further research uncovered the almost-lost-to-posterity suggestion that the winner of the opposing views should be determined the old-fashioned way: duke it out, toe-to-toe like men's men. The *code duello*. Honor above retreat.

Ptolemy went about five feet three and hit the scales in his birthday suit at around 105 pounds. A scrappy guy with a classic Greek athletic heritage. Copernicus was an inch or two taller and carried a bit more thickness provided by his eastern European birth and heartier calorie-laden cuisine.

Didn't happen. These were men of science. There was no fight. The laboratory was their sporting arena, the cosmos their everyday workplace, not the barroom floor where men and (to be historically even-handed and politically sensitive) women of less learning sometimes settle differences. Holy cow, how could you give even the slightest thought to the idea that these two brilliant men (one more brilliant than the other...or at least luckier) would stoop to a boxing match to win their way to fame? Get a grip.

Jonah And The Whale

This is an Ob-servation on the guy who is the eponym for one who brings bad luck. The word, his name, is from a book of the bible that relates the story of Jonah, a Jewish prophet. Trying to be faithful to the narrative, yet aiming for economy, I shall capsulize the story of Jonah to help illustrate the derivation of the word.

So this guy – his name is Jonah – is sitting there one day having a cool one under a tree and this big voice – actually it's God's – says, "Go down to Nineveh and cry against it" because there's a bunch of wickedness there. So Jonah gets out a map to see where Nineveh is. He is here in Israel, Nineveh is over there in Persia, and Tarshish is way down there. Nineveh?-Tarshish? Nineveh?-Tarshish? Tarshish!

So he goes to Joppa. Wait! Joppa's on the coast. Yes, but he's got to go there first to get on a boat for Tarshish, figuring God won't be looking for him there. Yeah, right. It doesn't work because God sees him and blows up this big storm with wind and rain and such and the boat is about to be broken. Whereat all of Jonah's shipmates are afraid, which is no big surprise. They cry out to their own gods and also decide to cast the vessel's wares overboard – thus creating the word jetsam – to lighten the boat. All this time, Jonah has been down below taking a nap. This is true; it's in the bible!

And the captain came to Jonah and said, "What meanest thou, O, sleeper? Arise, call upon thy God, if so be that God will think upon us, that we perish not." We don't know if Jonah understood any of this because he said nothing.

Instead, his shipmates recommended they "cast lots" to see who caused this turmoil. God was not a suspect. They go "eeny-meeny" and Jonah loses. It is not his day. They interrogate him and learn by deft questioning that he is "an Hebrew" and he fears "the Lord God of Heaven, which hath made the sea and dry land." And well he should fear for he's had lousy luck on both and it's about to get worse.

Jonah's shipmates are really scared now and have more questions, but they don't learn anything new. All they know is that "the sea wrought and was tempestuous." Then Jonah owns up to them, and he said unto them, "Take me up and cast me forth into the sea; so shall the sea be calm unto you, for I know that for my sake this great tempest is upon you." They think it over and decide instead to row like mad to get back to shore. Apparently they haven't been paying enough attention because "the sea wrought and was tempestuous against them." Still.

They were finally out of questions so they "cried unto the Lord" and said "we beseech thee" more than once. They didn't want to die on account of Jonah's having a tiff with the Lord. Then, after a light went on over their heads (an idea had occurred to them) they threw Jonah overboard. The sea calmed. To show their gratitude, they feared the Lord exceedingly, offered a sacrifice and made vows.

A whale ate Jonah.

Now you might think the story ends here. You are mistaken. Jonah had one of those epiphanies wherein he sees choices clearly distinguished between right and wrong. As he was in the belly of a whale, he chose wisely. Before that, however, he cried unto the Lord who heard him. After listening for a while, reportedly three days and three nights, God stuck his finger down the throat of the whale and, guess what, it hurled and out came Jonah.

God wasn't through with Jonah, or Nineveh for that matter, because this dubious city was still a rock in God's sandal. He says to Jonah for the second time, "Arise, go unto Nineveh, that great city, and preach unto it preaching that I bid thee."

Arise Jonah did. This time he's a bit smarter and doesn't head for Tarshish. He goes straight to Nineveh. The 3-day trip takes him only one day, pretty fast considering the time he needed to wash off three days and three nights of sojourning in a whale's bowels.

So he's in Nineveh and he says, "Yet 40 days and Nineveh shall be overthrown." These are powerful words, penetrating the intellect of the entire population down to the roots of their wickedness, for everyone, upon hearing these few words from Jonah, "believed God, proclaimed a fast, and put on sackcloth." Even the king participated, who himself also adorned sackcloth and sat in ashes.

In Nineveh, no one was eating, everyone went the sackcloth rage, water was outlawed, and they all were crying "mightily unto God" anticipating his next step. He said okay, I won't do any of that bad stuff for Nineveh that I'd planned. Upon hearing this, Jonah flipped. He was exasperated by all his expensive wanderings, his *mal de mers*, the belligerence of his fellow sailors, and (not mentioning that episode with the whale) his embarrassment before the Lord. He says, "Therefore now, O Lord, take, I beseech thee, my life from me, for it is better for me to die than to live." God answers, "Is it right for you to be angry?" This must be a trick question because Jonah needs to deliberate. He chooses a sunny spot over in East Nineveh, where he builds a shelter from the sun.

Jonah's new friend, God, sends over a gourd for more shade. Jonah's new friend is also a practical joker. The next morning he sends over a worm to smote the gourd. That meant the sun was beating down on Jonah. The "vehement east wind" prepared by God didn't help matters either, and now Jonah was really perplexed. He faints. But Jonah has enough clarity left to announce, again, his wish to die, proclaiming, "It is better for me to die than to live." The story ends with a conversation between God and Jonah:

G: "Is it right for you to be angry about the gourd?"
J: (Yes.)
G: "You have had pity on the gourd for which you have not labored and didn't make it grow, and which came up in a night and perished in a night."
J: "Huh?"

G: "And should I not spare Nineveh, that great city where there are more than 120,000 people who cannot discern between their right hand and their left hand…and also much cattle?"
Swear to God!

Garden Games

"I'm bored."

"Bored? You live in Eden for heaven's sake. How can you be bored?"

"How does one explain how one is bored? One is just bored," Eve said to Adam.

"That's crazy talk. Wanna play a game? Games don't bore you."

"I don't know. What game?"

"Tag."

"You always say tag."

"You like tag."

"No, you like tag. How about we play hide and seek?"

"Ha! Last time we played hide and seek you were gone for three days. That was no fun for me. God knows where you were hiding for three days."

"YOU GOT THAT RIGHT."

"Oh, it's him again."

"YES, IT'S ME AGAIN. AND I KNOW EVERYTHING. I KNOW WHERE YOU WERE HIDING."

"Do you know why she's bored?"

"WHAT DID SHE SAY?"

"She says it can't be explained. Boredom. One is just bored, she says."

"SOUNDS RIGHT TO ME. FREE WILL AND ALL THAT."

"Excuse me, but do you have to shout so? It hurts my ears."

"THIS IS MY VOICE."

"Maybe, but loud, let me tell you."

"OKAY. How's this, I'm whispering?"

"Oh, much better. Thank you."

"No problem. Why don't you guys play a game? I've noticed you both like games. Especially tag. I like to watch you play tag."

"You see, even he likes tag. Let's play tag."

"He likes it, does he? No kidding. It's a man thing."

"Come on, let's play tag. Keep him happy, too."

"I CAN HEAR YOU."

"Oh, sorry."

"Okay, I forgive you. Hey, forgiveness, that's my job, isn't it?"

"I guess."

"YOU DON'T HAVE TO GUESS. I JUST TOLD YOU. FORGIVENESS IS MY JOB. THAT SHOULD SETTLE IT."

"Yes, of course. Well, Eve, what about tag?"

"All right, let's have it your way and play tag, but we're going to have some new rules."

"You and your rules."

"New rules or we don't play. Got it?"

"Yes, dear."

"First rule, you don't touch me between my belly button and my collar bone. You're always trying for these."

"Oh, come on. What's the big deal? It's just for fun, you know."

"Not for me. Second rule, you don't tag me down here."

"What?!? Now you're going to spoil the whole game."

"Again, not for me."

"Holy cripes."

"WATCH IT."

"What? Watch what?"

"WHAT YOU SAID."

"All I said was holy cripes."

"Oh, I thought I heard you say something else. Go on. Play tag."

"What about you, Mr. I-like-tag. You have any rules?" Eve asked Adam.

"Tee hee. I would, but I'm sure you wouldn't follow my rule."

"Oh, Adam, grow up."

"DON'T COUNT ON IT. BOYS DON'T TEND…oops, sorry, my voice. Boys don't tend to grow up as you say."

"What boys are you talking about? We don't see any."

"You will. Oh, mercy, you will."

"Where are they now?"

"All that will happen soon enough. Let's not get ahead of ourselves. Back to tag. Who's it?"

At that prompting Eve delivered a blow to Adam's forehead with the heel of the palm of her hand. "You're it," she challenged as she ran off under the interested gaze of Adam and the Other One. Not far off, coiled in a tree – an apple tree the evidence suggests – a serpent was eyeing the whole affair. You could almost see in his eyes how he was scheming. "This is going to be so easy," he hissed to himself.

It Ain't Dante

"Once upon a time." Try diagramming that! You'll need a jackhammer and a crowbar to do it to give it any structural sense. What does it mean anyway? Maybe your 5-year-old gets it. However, most people are not going to confuse that line of literature with something from Dante. What they will get from the opening line – "Once upon a time" – is something that appears to have been conceived in the Ninth Ring of Hell. Violence, horror, abuse, you name it…all in the name of children's lit. They're called "fairy tales."

What do you get after you sit in your dad's lap and hear him read a fairy tale to you? Well, experience with almost all dads and all children is rampant. You get a nightmare. If you remain unconvinced, here is an abbreviated version of a famous fairy tale to set your blood racing toward a night of terror.

Once upon a time – there it is again – a couple prayed for a baby. After they discovered that wasn't working, they tried the conventional approach and she got with child. The momma-to-be saw some rampion, a sort of tur-nip, in a garden and wanted it. There was a high wall and the inevitable enchantress (There were loads of witches in the old days) "dreaded by all," and a slow-witted husband who needed prodding to do her bidding.

"But I'm pregnant," she said. He went and got some rampion. She liked it, so he went again. He got caught by the witch. He says to her that his wife needs it. The enchantress said, "Okay, but you'll suffer for it. Give me the baby when it's born." "Okay," says the husband, who doesn't even think about punching her out. The baby is born and, whoosh, here appears the enchantress. She takes the baby. If you haven't noticed by now, the enchantress is a really bad witch. (Today, we call this activity a kidnapping, and it is not the typical theme of children's art.)

The enchantress names the baby Rapunzel. The baby grows into a beautiful 12-year-old. Twelve! She also has long hair, really long hair. She lives in a tower. Towers are pretty trendy back then. The rule is only the enchantress can visit the girl. To do this, she calls out, "Rapunzel, Rapunzel, let down your hair to me." She climbs up the hair. (Is your child still awake listening to this?)

Time passes, naturally, and along comes a guy on a white horse, the king's son. He hears a song, he learns about the hair ladder, he climbs up and he proposes. Yes, she says; the girl, that is. A happy ending in prospect! No, because the silly girl spills the beans to the enchantress who cuts off all of Rapunzel's hair. The witch also sends the girl to a desert where she has to live in grief and misery. Then the evil woman intercepts the prince. She says something like, "You would take her away, but she no longer sings in her nest. The cat will scratch your eyes out." (Does your child have a cat?)

The king's son jumps out of the window. He lands in some thorns, which pierce his eyes. Blind, he wanders about for many years. (Question: where's his old man, the king, and all his legions?)

Now the prince is wandering all over the landscape until one day he hears familiar singing. He stumbles toward it and, sure enough, it's Rapunzel, living in wretchedness with her twins, a boy and a girl. She sees him and cries in his arms and the tears restore his sight. Rapunzel marries the nameless prince and they live for a long time, happy and content…and damn rich. He is, after all, son of a king.

The question that lingers, however, is where'd those twins come from.

The Labourer Who Wrought

You know that "wrought" is the past tense of work. It's what you would have done had you been hired to labor, say, in a vineyard. And today you could count your blessings, because, the statute of limitations notwithstanding, you could now be part of a potentially lucrative class action lawsuit. It was filed in the World Court under *Idle Labourers in the Marketplace v. Goodman of the Vineyard*. It challenges an old dodge that the law community has finally caught up to. We reproduce some of the relevant testimony to help the reader get a stronger grasp of "wrought." The history lesson will be valuable as well. It is, after all, biblical. The testimony continues from a swearing in.

Labourer (L): I do.
Plaintiff's Attorney (PA): You are a labourer, usually idle in a marketplace?
L: I am.
PA: You are willing to work – and have wrought – on a day-hire basis?
L: I am and I have.
PA: This would represent your livelihood, how you make ends meet?
L: It does.
PA: You have no other income?
L: I do.
PA: You do?
L: Yes, I do have no other income.
PA: Ah! (Pause.) Will you please tell the court how it happened that you were hired by Mr. Goodman?
L: Who?
PA: Mr. Goodman.
L: Oh, you mean the good man.
PA: Whatever. Please proceed.
L: Sure. I was idle that day, hanging around the marketplace wolfing the girls and…
PA: Sir?
L: Wolfing the gir…
PA: Skip over that part, it is unnecessary.

L: Okay. Well, I was in the marketplace, you know, waiting for the good man to hire me and my friends.

PA: The good man?

L: Yes, there's always some good man who wants to hire us for something. Do you want me to talk about some of the things we're hired for? We don't always gather grapes.

PA: Uh, no, just tell us about Mr. Goodman.

L: All right. Well, he comes by when he needs labourers in his vineyard. For him, we gather grapes. He makes wine. We get a penny a day.

PA: What?!?! A penny a day?

L: Yes.

PA: That's not very much.

L: It's the going rate.

PA: How many hours did you work for that penny?

L: Twelve.

PA: That's a long day for a penny.

L: A penny earned is a penny saved.

PA: Pithy. Now, after you had wrought for a few hours, didn't more labourers get hired? Tell us about that.

L: Well, the good man, he goes out about the third hour and more labourers show up. Then he does the same at the sixth hour and the ninth hour. We were up to here in labourers, let me tell you. Everyone was filling baskets with grapes and then at the eleventh hour he goes out again and more labourers show up. We work another hour and it's quitting time.

PA: You were there the whole day. Twelve hours.

Defense Attorney (DA): Objection! The plaintiff's attorney continues to put words in the witness's mouth.

Judge (J): Those words are already in the record, so I'll sustain.

PA: Sorry, your honor. Go ahead, please.

L: Yeah, twelve.

PA: And you were paid how much?

DA: Objection! Asked and answered.

PA: I am moving toward an important point.

DA: So does a snail, but this line of questioning is taking all day.

PA: Precisely, all day, and that is the point toward which I am moving.

J: Boys, boys, stay calm. I'll overrule on the assumption you are not a snail.

PA: Thank you, your honor. And your pay was?

L: A penny.

PA: When Mr. Goodman paid the labourers who joined you at the third and sixth and ninth and eleventh hours, how much were they given?

L: A penny. I read later that "we all received every man a penny."

PA: But you wrought so much more than they. What did you say to Mr. Goodman?

L: "These last have wrought but one hour, and thou hast made them equal unto us, which have borne the burden and heat of the day."

PA: Well said. What sayeth Mr., er, how did Mr. Goodman respond?

L: He said, "Friend…"

PA: Hah!

DA: Objection! This is a courtroom and it deserves more decorum than plaintiff's attorney is showing.

J: Sustained. Get on with it.

PA: Sorry, your honor. Proceed, please.

L: He said, "Friend, I do thee no wrong. Didst not thou agree with me for a penny?"

PA: Did you get it in writing?

L: No. Hardly anyone could write anyway. He just stopped by the market-place in his mule-drawn wagon and we'd yell and wave and he'd point at one of us and we'd jump in the back.

PA: You're in a union, correct?

L: Yeah, the International Idle Labourers. It's big. Millions of members. We get more every year.

PA: Whatever. Did you file a grievance?

L: Yes, with our steward.

PA: And?

L: Our steward ran off with the wife of one of the local's vice presidents. Never heard about it again.

PA: Back to Mr. Goodman. What else did he say?

L: He gabbed a bit then said, "So the last shall be first, and the first last. For many are called, but few are chosen."

PA: What did he mean by that?

L: I don't have a clue.

PA: Now, you know Mr. Goodman, right?

L: A little.

PA: Would you point him out?

L: What?

PA: Mr. Goodman. Point him out to the court.

L: But…

PA: But nothing. Just point at him.

L: I can't.

PA: Why not?

L: He's not here.

PA: Oh, and why not?

L: Well, because he's been dead for almost 3,000 years.

Three Wise Men

No animals were harmed during the writing of this Ob-servation if you do not count the two goats found under the tires of the caterer's truck and the limp in one of the camel's legs nobody noticed all morning while it grazed in a nearby field before a scene it would be needed in, which is where we enter as those three royals you've heard told of are riding west and a bit north, I think.

"Whose idea was this anyway? I'm freezing my ass off." "Stop your bellyaching, you signed up for it, don't forget, just like us." "Yeah."

The three Wise Men rode on.

For it came to pass a couple of millennia ago that someone in a governing post raised taxes and demanded payment at a tax station where the citizens had been born. You were to go there and pay your assigned levy. All this under the guise of a census. You don't really believe that Augustus Caesar called for a "census" to be paid for out of his own pocket, do you?

Furthermore, being a governor with a sense of humor, he chose December for the payment ritual. Before electric heat and paved highways. Funny.

Herod heard about it, too. Politicians, successful ones that is, do not let important decrees go unnoticed. Herod bided his time.

And it came to pass that the Baby Jesus was born in a manger, son of Joseph and the Virgin Mary. Rumors flew. Herod stopped biding his time. Previously, Joe and Mary, heavy with child (Mary, not Joe) had ridden on an ass to Bethlehem to fill in the census papers. That's where the manger was. That's where Joseph hailed from.

"Are you sure that's the right star, there are so many of them?" "He said the 'eastern star' and it would show us the way." "Is he an astronomer? No, I don't think so." "Just count your own lucky stars that there are no clouds tonight."

The three Wise Men rode on.

It had come to pass, see, that Herod needed someone to go over to Bethlehem and check out the kid who had been prophesied as a very special child. "Who shall we send?" asked one of his plenipotentiaries, whom his associates called "flunky." Not because Herod was a dull-witted infanticidal scoundrel, but rather that he hadn't thought about it is why he answered, "Who?"

Answering a question with a question is almost always poor form. Answering a question ("Who?") with the same question ("Who?") as in this case was downright boneheaded. Recovering, Herod said, "Get some volunteers. Maybe send twenty-five or thirty able riders. That ought to do the trick."

The outspoken flunky – plenipotentiary – inquired, "Do what? What do you want these two dozen or thereabouts able riders to do?" As a professional politician, Herod was a paragon and was quick with his answer. "I'm a politician, I kiss babies. Bring the bra…bring the child to me so that I may emblazon him with my lips." (It is not for this kind of talk alone that Herod's historical reputation is tarnished.)

The word went out throughout Judea that the king needed able camel-men to sign up for a journey. As it was December, the local patriotic fervor was chilly. There were no volunteers. Herod's first reaction was to fire his re-election campaign manager. He did that. His second was to resort to one of a politician's most effective arguments. He offered bribes. The money was to come from the state treasury, which in this case was also Herod's treasury.

The Three Kings of Orient understood Herod's political argument as sure as anyone. They are, after all, called "Wise Men" and they themselves had often indulged in the bribe stratagem when, it is reliably recorded, murder and mayhem did not serve their immediate interests. They took the bribes. They didn't need to take an IQ test to prove just how wise they were. Herod was satisfied.

The three Wise Men rode on. And so it came to pass...blah blah blah.

Bell's Telephone

It's been an awfully long time since Alexander Graham Bell invented the telephone. Don't look it up, it has. It was written down by somebody and that's my point. What do we really know about this bird? How do we know he did all the things he says he did? Besides that, I always thought that Edison fellow was our inventor. Goes to show.

They made a movie about Bell and his claims about the telephone, and I would not be knocked off my feet to learn that the movie was not entirely true to the facts. Movies can be like that. There are possibly books about all this, too, but I haven't seen one.

This thing about voices going over electrical wires in 1876 interests me. Did they even have electricity in Massachusetts? If so, why didn't they have night baseball?

Now let's move on to this Mr. Watson business. The first phone call is supposed to be from Bell to his assistant (Mr. Watson). "Watson, come here, I want you." Where's the evidence? Does Bell have a phone bill to prove it? What did Watson do? There is no record of that. How do we know that Watson didn't reply, "Hold on, Alex, I'm on the other line with my broker. I'm buying a hundred shares of AT&T. Looks like a good bet. Do you want in?"

Watson was in the room next to Bell. Who places a call to have "Watson come here" from the next room? A bit excessive. Our man Edison would have simply walked to the door and said, "Watson, come here, I want you." (It's true that Edison probably didn't know Mr. Watson, but you get my drift.) Moreover, the invention Edison was working on at the time – no matter what it was – is likely to have led to a lot less headache than the telephone that Bell says he invented.

Here's why. It's not in that movie about Bell, but I am confident that within a year or two Bell was ruing the day he dialed up Watson.

Here's why. Prank calls. Ring, ring. "Hello, Bell here, can I help you?" "Yes, do you have Prince Albert in a can?" "I beg your pardon." "Well, you better let him out. Tee-hee, tee-hee." "Rotten kids." (Bell should have invented Caller ID right away so he could track down these delinquents.)

So, we have covered a bit of ground in this Ob-servation, laying out some hypotheses, asking some questions, challenging the status quo. Next we're going to take a hard look at the real story behind the germ theory of communicable diseases and the moneyed interests that drive pharmaceutical companies and tort lawyers who blame the germs. This story is even older than this Bell telephone nonsense.

To Ply

To ply is to assail with vigor; to keep supplying or offering to someone. The following examination of "ply" derives from Genesis, so it comes not only with historical currency, but also with a measure of divine underpinnings. You use your own judgment whether and how you will in future use the word ply.

Two angels show up in the evening, and Lot is sitting at the gate of Sodom. He bows and scrapes. "Come to my house for the night, wash your feet," he says to them. They've been hiking a while. No, they say. He presses them, and they relent. Meanwhile, the men of the city, young and old, show up with demands, shouting to Lot to bring forth the two because they want to "know" them. This is, after all, Sodom. Anyway, Lot says no, don't do this wicked thing.

Instead, Lot offers up his two daughters, both virgins. "I have two daughters who have not had intercourse with men. Let me bring them out to you and you may do as you please. But don't do anything to these men, for they have come under the shadows of my roof." What a dad!

The men of Sodom demurred from such an invitation. This is, after all, Sodom. There was nearly a tussle, and the door closed, but not before the angels smote the men with a blinding light. The smotees are unable to reach the doorway. Then the angels tell Lot to gather all his relatives and to leave Sodom because they aim to destroy it. With God's help. Lot carries this message to his daughters' fiancés, who think he is kidding. The idiots. No amount of talk can change their minds. He apparently does not ply his argument hard enough.

Next the angels tell Lot to take his wife and daughters and leave Sodom, and oh, by the way, don't look back. Lot does not ask why. More tellingly, Lot's wife does not ask why. On the other hand, Lot argues about how far he should be expected to go. After some negotiations, it is agreed they need to go only as far as Zoar.

As they reach Zoar, the sun is rising. It is also the hour that God rains upon Sodom and Gomorrah, Sodom's equally iniquitous twin city, fire and brimstone. Brimstone is sulfurous stuff and is pretty awful. Fire you probably already know about. Lot's wife, being forgetful, looks back. She is turned into a pillar of salt. She's gotta think this is unfair. One little warning, and off-handed at that: "By the way, don't look back." A pillar of salt!

Abraham makes an appearance to check out the battle damage. Sure enough, God had sufficient ordnance to level Sodom and Gomorrah.

Do not be misled by the morals made and the good lessons learned so far. There's more. For the benefit of younger readers and scholars, it is only fair to tell you that the remainder of this tale earns an X rating. I will try to re-tell it with a delicate brushing.

Lot and his two daughters are now living in a cave "up from Zoar." The older daughter says to the younger, "Our father is old, and there is not a man on Earth to come in unto us after the manner of all the Earth." The younger one understands what this means. It's sort of like girl talk. "Come let us ply our father with wine and then lie with him that we may preserve seed of our father." So that night they ply their father with wine and the older daughter goes in and…well, enough said. A bit influenced by the wine, the father does not know what happens.

The next night, the conspiring daughters ply their father with more wine and the younger daughter takes her turn. The girls each had boys. They named them Moab and Ammon.

Ply is still a useful verb in its place. The behavior of the daughters in this story, on the other hand, is, it is hoped, frowned on today.

Seven

Seven is the same number of Cardinal Virtues as there are Deadly Sins. In the 10th century, Opening Day of the Dark Ages, during a heated debate in the campaign of good vs. evil being conducted in the cities and countryside of Europe, the Middle East, Asia, the sub-continent and other areas of the then-known populated world, Virtue and Sin met on a broad field of combat where, someone said, there would be more seating for ticket-holders, to settle the ancient argument: which had pre-eminence.

It was determined by a four-man umpiring crew that the seven virtues would be pitted against the seven sins in a winner-take-all bout of king of the hill. This was before kick-boxing, but not before some contestants…well, you will see.

This Ob-servation describing the contest is somewhat edited from a transcript that your enterprising correspondent discovered after following many leads from generally good sources. We plunge right in.

Charity and Envy went first. Envy being very strong, it prevailed in the early moments until Charity gathered its well-known human-interest into an offensive thrust and pushed Envy down the hill. The attending crowd whistled and shouted.

Anger and Justice climbed to the top. This one was over very quickly as Justice opened with a rhetorical assault. Anger listened briefly then punched Justice so hard it could not maintain its foothold on the hill. Anger won.

Prudence and Sloth were next. Side betting was heavy on Prudence to overcome its sedentary adversary. Much less, but smarter, money came down on Sloth, a human characteristic so manifestly widespread that some sociologists and neo-geneticists are coming to believe it is part of the building blocks of our nature. Prudence showed early skills but had no chance vs. the ability of Sloth to avoid hard work, thus saving its strength. Prudence did not prevail.

Two long shots came next. Covetousness faced Hope. Covetousness, distracted by...well, you know...slipped and went off the hill, Hope advancing.

The next contest was clearly lop-sided as Lust met Fortitude. Many who watched wondered why Fortitude even made it among the so-called Cardinal Virtues. No one questioned whether Lust was qualified as a Deadly Sin. Lust won this one easily, as it does in nearly all instances when a choice can be made.

When Temperance defeated Gluttony in the succeeding match, some observers raised an eyebrow or two, but the record shows Gluttony was not in good competitive shape.

Faith and Pride, two of the favorites, drew byes in the first round, leaving eight combatants.

The crowd watching the matches swelled as word spread and people from far-off communities made their way to within eyesight of the hill. Many, it should be noted, were unacquainted with the surviving virtues and sins. Some even confessed that they did not know the difference among the behaviors striving for ascendancy. "How can there be Justice without Anger?" some asked. "What is Fortitude without a proportion of Sloth?" "Am I condemned by my Pride?" "Where can I get more Lust?"

The contest between good and evil had attracted ever more people and was taking on an air of a great spectacle. Invariably, it promoted side events. For example, ministrants and their deacons and subalterns drew spectators to hastily organized religious services to deplore the competing sins and exhort the virtues. Not far away and out of sight in tents, others with different enterprises in mind were earning easy money by playing to the urgings of one of the better-known deadly sins.

The second round of the competition resumed with Charity and Anger on the hill. Charity, the underdog and showing some fear, resorted to the argument that its precedence was more deserving because of its effects on others, including even those who had no interest in its beneficence. This pissed off Anger, which momentarily left it just beyond self-control, in which moment Charity ungraciously kicked Anger in his shin. Anger, angry, yelled as he grasped the painful spot with both arms hoping about on one leg, leading Charity to the cowardly but tactically advantageous answer. He shoved his opponent who tumbled down the hill. Charity offered apologies to the throng that had to witness this uncharacteristic but not ineffective display. The throng didn't seem to care one way or the other.

Lust and Temperance, contestants in the next show, were off the books by the odds makers. It was nearly a walkover for Lust. Temperance didn't stand a chance. When it was over, lots of spectators went looking for the several places where the winning enterprise was being satisfied.

Many others in the crowd used the next match – an uninspiring setup between Sloth and Hope – to make a run for the trenches. The scuttlebutt was that the match to follow this one was to be a pip, i.e. Faith vs. Pride, so everyone wanted no barking from their bowels or their bladders. Sloth, still recovering from its overtaxing first round elimination of Prudence, did not show well and fell off the hill, Hope advancing again.

Like two gladiators, Faith and Pride climbed the hill, one on each side, accompanied not by cheering and jeering but by a hushed awe. These were two of the strongest human forces and were known to the spectators with intimacy. The winner would establish a dominance that was expected to spell the eventual supremacy of the day. Who could challenge man's faith, who its pride? At the top of the hill, Faith bowed slightly to Pride, Pride acknowledging the honor with a silent, motionless disdain, contemptuous of its opponent in its unbreakable spirit.

Pride moved toward Faith and the crowd froze in anticipation. Pride stopped. It asked Faith, "Is it possible for us to co-exist, to be vested together in a single person full of himself or herself, with a need for reliance on no other person or no other succor?" Faith replied, "You can exist by relying on what you cannot see, for this righteous blindness fills our lives and through it we will triumph and earn our shares in eternity." "I cannot have pride *and* faith?" "Faith must supercede pride."

From out of the crowd someone shouted, "Is it okay to have faith and lust; I'd go along with that." Those around shouted down the interruption.

Pride continued. "I propose that you show me the strength of faith by being prideful of yourself as well as your trust in what you cannot see." Faith replied, "I counter that you show me proof for pride while bearing your faithlessness in what you cannot see."

The man in the crowd shouted again, "How about hope and lust?" This time the people near him ran him off a good many paces.

"I am unconvinced by your proposal," Faith said. "And I am un-swayed by yours," Pride answered. "It remains," Faith said, "for the weaker to descend." Pride said, "I bid you farewell." The spectators gasped and the excitement rippled in every direction from the hill that the contest was ended. A moment passed and then down the hill's slope walked Faith.

The sun was lowering when with a common realization the large numbers attending this spectacle decided they had not eaten and were hungry. In the crowd, a man had brought some loaves of bread and some fishes, prepared, unlike the others, for a longer day. They looked at him. He ate the fish and chewed the bread. The others remained hungry.

Two virtues – Charity and Hope – and two sins – Lust and Pride – awaited resumption of the challenge. Then the crowd saw Charity and Pride climb to the top of the hill. "We are much alike, I aver," Pride said. "What! You slander me," Charity charged. "Ah, no," Pride said, "we are both so giving of our desires." "But I give so that others may be refreshed from want or misery," said Charity. "And I am one of those," spoke Pride which quite un-valiantly pushed Charity down the hill. Few if any in the crowd felt surprise at this outcome. Pride had too much going for it.

Few, also, had doubts about the way the other semi-final would conclude. Lust vs. Hope was a mismatch. The crowd was restless, uninterested in this obvious elimination of Hope from the contest.

"Bring on the sins," some chanted, anticipating a gargantuan encounter between Lust and Pride. Hope, looking hopeful, and Lust, leering, climbed their way to the top. "I am armed," Lust snapped at Hope, "with the primal drives that make me indispensable. Without me there is no future for the human race." "You are, on the contrary," Hope said, "the rocky path to unhappiness. With you, there is no reason for the human race." "Do you expect me to withdraw without a fight?" Lust sneered. "I make no such demand," Hope replied, "but as there is room only for one of us to go forward, it cannot be you, for where your perseverance is toward a goal within your reach, and when obtained you are sated, if only temporarily, my perseverance is endless. I offer humankind not a temporary answer but unending expectation. You do not have enough days to overcome me." "Look at the tits on that woman over there," Lust shouted temptingly at Hope, hoping Hope's attention might be diverted sufficiently to allow a swift push down the hill. Hope did not turn, but sidestepped the lunging Lust who took a header over the crest of the hill. Hope advanced once again, this time to the ultimate challenge.

Uncounted thousands of people massed on the fields circumferencing the hill where virtue and sin were about to determine the superiority of the one septet over the other, or so it was proclaimed by an elder who crawled with difficulty to the top of the hill. "For all time the victors will prevail over the vanquished," he said, "and we plead with the Lord that He giveth strength to Hope that it may carry virtue to its rightful place above sin." He was an old elder, weak of voice, and only those near the base of the hill could hear his prayer. A different, but familiar, voice called out, "Give Lust another chance. Tell some of the women here to pull down their pants." This time two hearty souls – and big ones at that – gave the character a thrashing. Left with a slew of bruises and a bleeding nose, he limped off wiping blood from his chin. Not far away he stopped and called back toward the hill, "I thank God I did not call for Justice. My fate then would have been sealed by a failed virtue. And thank you, Temperance, for coming to my aid," he added sarcastically. "Piss off, asshole," someone yelled at him.

The swelling crowd became increasingly restless. Under an oak on the land, a band of raiders from the west were intimidating everyone around them, shouting epithets and splashing mead over observers nearby. "We came to see some fighting on the hill," one yelled, "and there's more of that down here than up there." "Nobody invited you," a woman dared. "Yeah," someone agreed, anonymously. Three of the raiders left the shade of the oak and went over to the woman and began kicking the poop out of her. They stopped when the crowd heaved with news that the two finalists were nearing the hill.

Pride swaggered forward through the people close to the hill, eyeing everyone with confidence. Hope, on the other side of the hill, looked up to the top and began climbing. Pride, hearing people calling for Hope, hurried to the top and got there first. "There is irony in your name," Pride said to Hope with derision. "I'll wager that you have none. In fact, I have wagered on myself and I intend to win and to profit today."

Hope said nothing. "Tell me," Pride went on, "what is it that brings you to this defeat? What weaklings have you fooled that I have such a feeble foe as you to send down and proclaim the uselessness of virtues?" "I would have more concern for my responsibility," Hope finally said, "if I could agree with the power you pretend, but as it is self-assigned, well…" Pride was briefly stymied before responding, "Multiply my power by the millions of people who put themselves above others in all places and in all times. There can be no superior power because there is no other reasoning animal in your God's kingdom. Reason dictates pride." Pride turned and grinned at the waves of people watching. Hope said, "Strip from people each of their goodnesses and their frailties; ask them to sacrifice what keeps them warm when in cold, fed when in want, consoled when in grief. Take away even their self-image. Naked in this way to nature, what is the one thing that they still hold on to?" "I know what you are trying to say," Pride said, "I have heard it before. Tell me, if you can, if ever a human being has gone without pride? Can you tell me, for example, if the modest or the meek have ever not been prideful at least of their abasement? I think not." "Pride goeth before a fall," Hope reminded its adversary. "Abandon all hope ye who are born of man," Pride said, somewhat out of context.

Neither spoke for a moment. Then the crowd heard, "There can be no victor, pride prevails universally, while hope always remains." No one knows for sure who spoke the words. At the top of the hill the two stared quietly, looking at one another with vanished expectation. Simultaneously, they turned slowly and climbed down opposite sides of the hill.

"Who won?" someone called out from the outer fringe of the crowd. "Virtue," came the answer. "No, no, it was sin." "Get serious, you jerk, it wasn't sin." "Sure it was, dickhead." And soon the arguing had enveloped the entire spectacle in a heck of a dustup. The debate has been continuing since and not without a lot of bloody noses, conquered territory, peace treaties and new churches.

The Rubicon

The Rubicon is a river in northern Italy or thereabouts. A small river, too, though big enough for Julius Caesar to celebrate his crossing of it with his famous proclamation, *"Veni, vidi, vici."* When asked what he meant by this, he answered, "By crossing the Po, I predict to the world my successful intentions against southern Italians." "This is not the Po," he was told. "Not the Po? How can that be?" "We crossed the Po three days ago. You were drunk." "Not the Po? Which river is this?" "This is the Rubicon." "The what?" "The Rubicon." "Never heard of it. When did we cross the Po, did you say?" "Three days ago, you know, on the Ides of March." "Oooh, don't remind me of that." One of his aides asked, "Caesar, what shall we do now?" Caesar thought for a moment and then said, "Well, what the hey! I'll cross the Rubicon." He happened to have a pair of dice in his vestments and threw one to the ground, saying, *"Iacta alea est."* That's Latin. Caesar spoke Latin. It means "the die is cast." Do you get it? Me neither.

The End

www.ingramcontent.com/pod-product-compliance
Lightning Source LLC
Chambersburg PA
CBHW070953040426
42443CB00007B/487